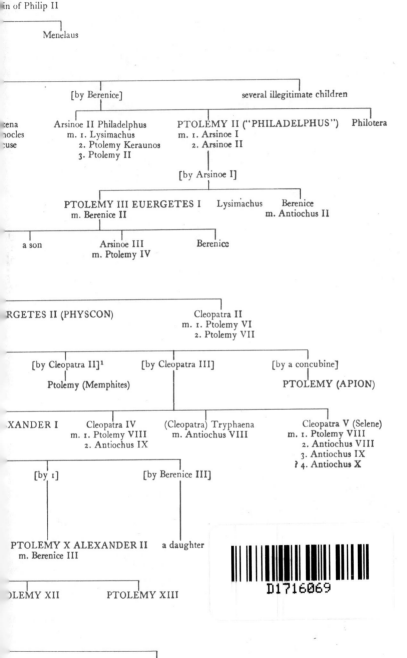

Vivian Coffman

Menelaus

[by Berenice]   several illegitimate children

kena   Arsinoe II Philadelphus   PTOLEMY II ("PHILADELPHUS")   Philotera
nocles   m. 1. Lysimachus   m. 1. Arsinoe I
cuse   2. Ptolemy Keraunos   2. Arsinoe II
       3. Ptolemy II

[by Arsinoe I]

PTOLEMY III EUERGETES I   Lysimachus   Berenice
m. Berenice II   m. Antiochus II

a son   Arsinoe III   Berenice
       m. Ptolemy IV

RGETES II (PHYSCON)   Cleopatra II
                 m. 1. Ptolemy VI
                 2. Ptolemy VII

[by Cleopatra II][1]   [by Cleopatra III]   [by a concubine]

Ptolemy (Memphites)   PTOLEMY (APION)

XANDER I   Cleopatra IV   (Cleopatra) Tryphaena   Cleopatra V (Selene)
       m. 1. Ptolemy VIII   m. Antiochus VIII   m. 1. Ptolemy VIII
       2. Antiochus IX   2. Antiochus VIII
                                   3. Antiochus IX
                                   ? 4. Antiochus X

[by 1]   [by Berenice III]

PTOLEMY X ALEXANDER II   a daughter
m. Berenice III

LEMY XII   PTOLEMY XIII

ne   Ptolemy Philadelphus
retania

of Mauretania

From Cambridge Ancient History, Vol. VII.
Copyright © 1954. Reprinted by permission of
Cambridge University Press.

D1716069

IN THE FINAL DAYS

By

WALTER K. PRICE

MOODY PRESS

CHICAGO

Library of Congress Cataloging in Publication Data

Price, Walter K
  In the final days.
  Bibliography: p. 183.
  1. Bible. O. T. Daniel XI—Criticism, interpretation, etc
I. Title.
BS1555.2.P74   224'.5'07   76-58907
ISBN 0-8024-4059-2

To my beloved friends
who make up
The First Baptist Church
Danville, Kentucky

Contents

Foreword

ANOTHER BOOK from the prolific pen of Walter K. Price is a welcome addition to the literature on prophecy. Although volumes regarding the prophetic elements in the Bible have leaped from the press, there are some genuine distinctives in this book, *In the Final Days*.

First, this effort is the result of careful study of the Scripture as the reader would have every right to expect. In addition, a theology is represented herein that has been hammered out not only behind the desk but also among the people of God. Walter Price, evangelist and Bible conference leader, presents a product bathed in the realities of life. This book presents the reflection of the scholar and the perspective of the evangelist.

Another remarkable adjunct about this book is that the author has arrived at these premillennial conclusions after a period of ardent support of amillennial, allegorical hermeneutic. Confrontation with the biblical text eradicated presuppositions and reestablished the naturalness of the literal method of interpretation.

Finally, the unique contribution of the book is in the scope of its inquiry. The author has limited himself to conscientious historical and exegetical investigation of the eleventh chapter of Daniel. The study of these prophecies and their relationship to Antichrist are inevitably subjects of great interest among Christians.

W. A. CRISWELL

Introduction

THE LITTLE VILLAGE of Kolville is somewhere in the Carpathian Mountains. It is 1920. A pogrom against the Jews is about to erupt. Moshe, a Hasidic master, is in prison. Though he is innocent, he has confessed to the crime of murdering a Christian youth, hoping that his confession will spare the Jewish community the wrath of a Christian mob. The rabbi's disciple comes to him in jail. Moshe refuses to teach his student anymore, whereupon the student reminds his master that Rabbi Akiba continued to instruct his students even though he had been imprisoned by the Romans and forbidden further teaching of the Torah. The parallel is so concise that the student recalls a statement which the Hasidic master himself had made, for Moshe had often observed that "nothing in Jewish tradition is unconnected. In Jewish history everything is linked."[1]

This principle of Jewish continuity is unique. This means that no event in past Jewish history can be isolated from the course of world events or from the Jew's own historical consciousness.

The Jew is a catalyst in these affairs. The Jews are a control in the archives of history, for they remain constant while all else changes. This Jewish persistence through the changing course of human affairs means that God has elected the Jew to a unique destiny, giving him an unprecedented position in world events. This is why God, in His original covenant with Abraham, said that whosoever blesses the Jew will

1. Elie Wiesel, *The Oath*, p. 186.

9

be blessed, and whosoever curses him will be cursed (Gen 12:3). Therefore, the Jew is the constant arbitrator of good or evil among all the Gentiles, for the course of the nations is set by their attitude toward the Jew.

Not only is the Jew an unchanging mystery in world affairs, but he also is the medium for propelling the course of world events toward a final goal, and it will be the Jews in whom end-time events will be consummated. The Greeks viewed history as moving in a circle, beginning nowhere and ending nowhere. But the Hebrew viewed history—and particularly their part in human history—as moving in a straight line toward an unalterable destiny. The Gentile world may flounder in its attempts to realize a meaningful place in current events, but Jewish history moves inexorably toward that destiny which the prophets marked out for the covenant people, a golden age in which their Messiah will rule the world in peace.

Not only is the destiny of the Jews prescribed by the prophets of Israel, but occasionally in their history, future events, which are also a part of their destiny, are foreshadowed in current happenings. Prototypes of things to come have occurred periodically in the Jewish experience, indicating that the future can break in upon the present. The recent Nazi holocaust is an example. During the holocaust era the Jews suffered as never before. However, their current plight becomes a prototype of Israel's last great episode of suffering, known in Bible prophecy as the Great Tribulation. In the Nazi era the Jews were threatened with genocide, yet they survived. However, the tendency to survive great persecution and the threat of genocide has surfaced many times in Jewish history—in the Egyptian bondage, during the Sennnacherib crisis, during the time of Queen Esther. The most dramatic prototype of the Great Tribulation, however, occurred during the reign of Antiochus IV Epiphanes in the second century B.C. In those days King Antiochus of Syria terrorized the Jews by attempting to force an alien religion upon them. He severely persecuted those who would not yield. Consequently, in those days, we have Jewish history's most profound rehearsal of the coming Great Tribulation.

In addition, the Jews of the second century B.C. Maccabean crisis, as well as those of all other holocaust events, reacted the same way when the Torah and the Temple were threatened by Gentile forces. The attitude of the Jews in the Roman persecutions, for example, reflects the Jewish attitude during the Maccabean crisis of 168-165 B.C. This also predicts what their attitude will be during their ultimate plight when the end days bring the Antichrist's persecutions.

The events of the Maccabean era preview the events of the last days which will surround the rise, reign, and demise of the Antichrist. Jesus called them the days of Great Tribulation (Matt 24:21). Daniel spoke of them in this vision. First, as the events of the last days would be foreshadowed in the reign of the Seleucid king, Antiochus IV Epiphanes (Dan 11:21-35); and second, as they will be actualized in the Antichrist's reign (11:36-45). Prior to his focusing upon Antiochus and the Antichrist in chapter 11, Daniel portrayed the Gentile dominion over the Jews which sets the stage for these events (11:1-20).

Daniel's vision begins with a prediction about the fall of the second great Gentile power, Persia (11:2).

The rapid rise and reign of Alexander the Great of Greece follows as the third Gentile world empire to dominate the Jews (11:3).

Next, Daniel saw the struggle for control of Alexander's empire, which erupted immediately after his death, in which four of the Greek generals emerged in control (11:4).

Then the long and indeterminate struggle between the Ptolemies of Egypt (king of the south) and the Seleucids of Syria (king of the north) is presented. Their political intrigues and military aggressions are depicted in a body of Scrip-

ture which has become the most tedious to explain in all of
Bible prophecy (11:5-20). Every expositor must enlist his
readers' patience as he attempts to shed light upon Daniel 11:
5-20.

Finally, Antiochus IV Epiphanes came to the throne of the
Seleucid Empire. He was destined to treat the Jews in such a
way as to win for himself an infamous place both in Scripture
and in Jewish tradition as the ultimate type of the evil Gentile ruler, the archenemy of God's people (11:21-35).

Daniel terminated his prophecy by merging his vision of
Antiochus with a preview of the coming Antichrist (11:36-45).

Daniel's vision in chapter 11 indicates that what will trans-
pire during the Great Tribulation has already been played
out upon the stage of Jewish history 2,200 years ago. The
prophet predicted the dominion of the Gentiles over the Jews,
beginning with the Babylonians, through the successive conquests of the Persians, Greeks, Egyptians, and Syrians. There
he stopped. Daniel did not foresee the Romans in chapter 11,
for Antiochus IV Epiphanes, the Seleucid king, epitomizes all
that the Antichrist will be during the end days. No Roman
persecutor of Israel was more diabolical than was King Antiochus, and none was as typical of what the Antichrist will be
as was this Seleucid king. Daniel's vision climaxes in a preview of King Antiochus, whose reign was a precursor of the
reign of the Antichrist.

The days of Antiochus IV Epiphanes contain historical
events predicted by Daniel. However, they transcend the second century B.C. and merge into the events of the last days and
the Great Tribulation. With no discernible break, Daniel
moves in his vision from the near future into the distant future, from Antiochus Epiphanes to the Antichrist, and from
the days of the Maccabees to the days of the Great Tribulation.

Therefore, it is the thesis of this exposition that in the second century B.C. a foreshadowing of the Great Tribulation oc-

curred in Israel. Observing its special features and the way that the Jews weathered its threats holds much instruction for that generation of Jews who will be contemporaries of the Antichrist and his evil designs upon them, which will threaten their very existence. The fact that Israel survived the pogroms of King Antiochus gives optimism to all future generations and especially to that generation of Jews who will be alive in the Great Tribulation period.

During the three and one half years between June 168 and October 165 B.C. the Jewish people experienced the epitome of the Great Tribulation. The future holocaust to come upon Israel was given historical precedent through the persecutions of King Antiochus. In those days this demented dictator of the Seleucid Empire imposed a dress rehearsal of end-time events upon the people of Israel.

A foreshadowing is a description of future events which are compressed into a given segment of history. The events, which involved the persecution of the Jews, the desecration of the Temple, and the great deliverance under Judas Maccabee, are due to be repeated in the last days. This similarity is too precise to have been contrived or to be merely coincidental.

Jesus gave us the key to this relationship between Antiochus IV Epiphanes and the Antichrist when He indicated that the days of the abomination of desolation are both historic and prophetic and are relevant to both the Maccabean era and the Great Tribulation.

Historically, the abomination occurred during the second-century B.C. tyrannical reign of Antiochus. Prophetically, the abomination will occur again during the reign of the Antichrist just before the Messiah's advent.

Apparently the horrors of the Great Tribulation period will be so devastating that they will necessitate a preview in actual history in order to indicate that survival is possible. The Lord not only has shortened those days (Matt 24:22), but He also has previewed them in order that the Jews will not be overcome with despair. Their forefathers overcame the threats of Antiochus IV Epiphanes, and their sons and daughters can endure the threats of the Antichrist and enter into the Messianic Kingdom. Therefore, the Lord has typified the events of the Great Tribulation period, causing them to be played out historically between 168 and 165 B.C. in the reign of King Antiochus.

Furthermore, just as the Passover points back to the deliverance of the Jews from Egyptian oppression, so the Jewish feast of Hanukkah is a reminder of the deliverance of the Jews from Syrian oppression. King Antiochus threatened the Jews with spiritual annihilation. So will the Antichrist. But the same God who delivered the Jews from the pogroms of Antiochus in 165 B.C. also will deliver the faithful remnant in Israel from the machinations of the Antichrist in the end days.

What is to happen has already happened. This is the theme of Daniel 11.

No other people have been granted a preview of coming events as have the Jews. This preview is encased in the verbal prediction of Daniel, whose prophetic preview was historically fulfilled in the second-century B.C. reign of King Antiochus. However, its larger fulfillment is yet to be realized in the final holocaust which is to come upon Israel, the Great Tribulation of which the Maccabean era is a foreshadowing.

In Daniel 11, the Maccabean era and the Great Tribulation join history and prophecy in a dramatic exposition of the redemption of Israel which will come during the end days from a greater Deliverer than Judas Maccabee. Consequently the events of the Great Tribulation already have been epitomized in the Maccabean era nearly 2,200 years ago.

Daniel predicted both in his vision.

1

The Rise and Fall of Alexander the Great

Daniel 11:2-4

Fulfilled: 334-323 B.C.

A SHOVEL invades the earth, breaking the silence of a lonely churchyard. Amid the clods, a skull is tossed up by the gravedigger. Two men approach. One of them retrieves this discarded skull. Contemplating it, Hamlet traces the fate of Alexander the Great to the infamy of dusty death.[1]

The influence of this mighty Greek king lives on, however. And to no group is this ancient conqueror more significant than to the Jews, for the conquest of Alexander the Great marked a turning point in their history. Heretofore, Israel's fate was determind by conquerors based in the east—Assyrians, Babylonians, Persians. But in the fourth century B.C. a new era was introduced in which all alien rulers of Israel would be westerners. The Jews, from the time of Alexander, have been threatened by western culture, first from the Greeks and then from the Romans.

Alexander, having heard of the strength, the valor, and the heroism of the Jews, traveled toward Palestine in order to conquer them. "For," said he, "if I do not defeat the Jews, all my glory is as nothing." Arriving at Dan, Alexander sent a messenger to Jerusalem demanding all of the Temple treasure. When the people received this message they were troubled. They prostrated themselves in sackcloth and prayed while the high priest answered Alexander's letter, saying that they would gladly pay tribute in gold to the great king, but

1. Shakespeare *Hamlet* 5.1.225-35.

15

they could not remove the vessels from the Temple which
their ancestors had consecrated. Alexander grew very angry
and swore by his idols that he would not depart from Jerusalem until the city and the Temple were reduced to rubble.
Then, to quote from the medieval Hebrew manuscript which
contains one version of this famous legend,

> During the night, as the king lay awake on his bed, he no-
> ticed through the open window of his tent an angel of God
> standing with a drawn sword.
> Terrified, the king exclaimed, "Why would my lord strike
> his servant?"
> The angel replies: "It is I who conquer kings for you, and
> trample nations beneath you. Why did you swear to do evil
> in the eyes of God by destroying His land and His people?"
> The king said, "Please my lord, I will do whatsoever you
> say."
> "Beware of your soul and do no harm to the people of
> Jerusalem," answered the angel dressed in linen, "but when
> you arrive there be concerned with their welfare, treat them
> well and deposit your treasures in the House of the Lord. If
> you disobey me, you and yours will die."
> Alexander said to the angel dressed in linen: "It is very
> difficult for me to humble myself in this way. However, if it
> displeases you, I will turn back and not enter Jerusalem."
> The angel answered: "Beware, lest you turn your back
> before coming to Jerusalem and bringing your treasures to
> the House of the Lord."
> Morning came. The king and his entire army arrived in
> Jerusalem. When he came before the gate of the city, he was
> welcomed by Annani, the High Priest, accompanied by
> eighty priests dressed in holy garments. They came to plead
> with him to spare the city. When Alexander saw Annani,
> the High Priest, he dismounted from his horse, and pros-
> trated himself before him, embracing and kissing the priest's
> feet.
> Alexander's warriors were displeased at this and said,

"Why do you do this? Why did you degrade yourself before this man? Dukes and lords have prostrated themselves before you, and now you have lowered yourself by descending from the chariot and bowing before this old man."

"Do not be amazed," said the King. "This old man who came toward me resembles the angel of God who leads me at the time of battle and who tramples nations beneath me. Therefore, I have bestowed all this honor upon him."[2]

Both Josephus and the Talmud report a similar incident in the experience of Alexander.[3] Josephus adds that from Mount Scopos, where this meeting is said to have taken place, Alexander was led in a gala procession down into the Temple. After he had offered sacrifices, the priests got out the scroll of Daniel and showed him the prophet's prediction about a Greek king's conquest of the Persian Empire (Dan 7:6; 8:3-8, 20-22; 11:3).

Alexander, they declared, was that king.

THE RISE OF ALEXANDER THE GREAT

Behold, there shall stand up yet three kings in Persia; and the fourth shall be far richer than they all: and when he is waxed strong through his riches, he shall stir up all against the realm of Greece. And a mighty king shall stand up, that shall rule with great dominion, and do according to his will (Dan 11:2-3).

This is one of the passages shown to the Macedonian king. Daniel predicted that Alexander the Great would emerge upon the stage of prophetic history in a conflict with the Persian Empire.

The prophet's vision indicates that it would be the Persians themselves who would create the circumstances out of which a

---

2. Rosalie Reich, *Tales of Alexander the Macedonian: A Medieval Hebrew Manuscript*, pp. 63-69.
3. Josephus *Antiquities* 11.8.3-5; cf. *Yoma* 69a; *Ta'anet* 9; *Midrash Rabbah* Gen. 60.1.7.

great king like Alexander would arise. Specifically, Daniel
marked out the fourth ruler of Persia whose wealth and con-
sequent might would encourage him to agitate Greece. It
would be in the context of this Persian aggression toward
Greece that Alexander the Great would come forth to curse
the Persian ruler.

This vision came to Daniel during the reign of Cyrus (10:
1). The four Persian kings mentioned in this prophecy have
been variously identified.[4] However, the next four kings to
reign after Cyrus seem to be the ones meant, especially since
the fourth in this sequence was Xerxes I whose great wealth
enabled him to invade Greece with a vast army and navy. He
was defeated at the Battle of Salamis on September 28, 480
B.C., and, with his defeat, the Persian Empire began its gradu-
al decline. Xerxes I is the Ahasuerus of the book of Esther
whose royal splendor represented the acme of Persian power.
His defeat by the Greeks was also the point at which Persia
began to decline. Other kings sat on the throne of Persia
after Xerxes I, but Daniel did not mention them, for Persia
was even then politically dead. Nevertheless, it continued as a
waning power for more than a century after that.

Daniel takes no note of subsequent Persian kings but passes
on to Alexander the Great.

In Daniel 11:2-3 the prophet speaks of a Persian provocation of Greece which calls forth Alexander the Great. The
actual chronology of events is not that concise, however.
Xerxes I provoked Greece, and then, many years later, Alexander the Great arose in Greece to take revenge upon Persia.
Though more than a century passed between the provocation
of Xerxes I and the rise of Alexander, Daniel portrays these
events in a cause and effect relationship. Xerxes's provocation
of Greece caused Alexander the Great to take his revenge up-

4. The four kings whom most conservative scholars identify are Cambyses
(529-522 B.C.); Pseudo-Smerdis (522 B.C.); Darius I (522-486 B.C.);
and Xerxes I (486-465 B.C.).

on Persia. However, 131 years actually separated the death of Xerxes from Alexander's resulting invasion.

Philip of Macedon, Alexander's father, had become ruler of all Greece in 338 B.C. Further conquests in Thrace brought the borders of Philip's expanding empire up against the Persian provinces in western Asia Minor. War with Persia was inevitable.

In 336 B.C., while preparing for war with the Persian Empire, Philip of Macedon was assassinated by one of his officers.

Philip's son, Alexander, followed his father on the throne at the age of twenty. Immediately things began to change. Philip of Macedon wanted only to secure his rule over all Greece and to dominate the Straits of Hellespont, modern Dardanelles, in order to guarantee the trade routes between the Aegean Sea and the Black Sea. Macedonian strategy then took a radical turn, for Alexander was soon bent upon the destruction of the Persian Empire. His was a war of revenge upon Persia, which had been interfering in Greek affairs for more than a century.

At this point in history the driving force of Alexander's character was complemented by the military prowess of the Macedonian cavalry and infantry on the one hand and the political and military weakness of Persia on the other. Thus the stage was set for Alexander's conquests which would bring Palestine into the framework of western civilization and eventually engage the Jews with the most subtle threat their religion ever faced: Hellenism.

Several different passages in Daniel predict the swift advance of Alexander the Great. In one of Daniel's visions Alexander is an apocalyptic "he-goat" charging the Persian ram.

> And as I was considering, behold, a he-goat came from the west over the face of the whole earth, and touched not the ground: and the goat had a notable horn between his eyes. And he came to the ram that had the two horns, which I saw standing before the river, and ran upon him in the fury of

his power. And I saw him come close unto the ram, and he
was moved with anger against him, and smote the ram, and
brake his two horns; and . . . he cast him down to the ground,
and trampled upon him; and there was none that could
deliver the ram out of his hand. And the he-goat magnified
himself exceedingly (Dan 8:5-8).

In addition to this revelation, the kingdom which Alexander established is also previewed in Daniel's vision of the
great colossus in chapter 2 as the "third kingdom of brass,
which shall bear rule over all the earth" (2:39). In a similar
vision recorded in Daniel 7, the Greek empire of Alexander
is also represented by the third beast which arose from the
sea: "After this I beheld, and, lo, another, like a leopard,
which had upon its back four wings of a bird; the beast had
also four heads; and dominion was given to it" (7:6).

All of these verses were actually fulfilled in 334 B.C. when
Alexander the Great appeared at the northwest corner of Asia
Minor, followed by 35,000 troops.

The first encounter between the he-goat and the ram, Alexander and the forces of Persia, occurred in western Asia Minor
at the Granicus River. The Persians were defeated and the
whole of Asia Minor fell open to Alexander.

A year later, 333 B.C., Alexander faced King Darius III for
the first time at the gates of Syria. The king's army was defeated at Issus. However, the Persian king escaped, leaving
his family to be captured by the Greeks. It was after the battle of Issus, says Plutarch, that Alexander, "sent to Damascus
to seize upon the money and baggage, the wives and children,
of the Persians. . . . This first gave the Macedonians such a
taste of the Persian wealth and women and barbaric splendor
of living, that they were ready to pursue and follow upon it
with all the eagerness of hounds upon a scent."[5]

The next year, 332 B.C., found Alexander moving down

5. John Dryden, trans., *Plutarch: The Lives of the Noble Grecians and
   Romans*, p. 817.

the Syrian coast toward Egypt. The cities of the maritime plane yielded to him, with only Tyre and Gaza resisting. It took many months to break through Tyre's fortifications, while Gaza fell in a matter of sixty days and was razed to the ground by the Greeks.

Alexander's side trip to Jerusalem may have occurred at some point in his march toward Egypt, if Josephus is accurate.[6]

When he finally arrived in Egypt, the Persian satrap in charge yielded to him without a fight, and Egypt, which had never really regarded itself as a part of the Persian Empire, hailed Alexander as a liberator. He, in turn, treated the Egyptians with consideration. The Talmud says that the Egyptians even felt free to ask Alexander to force the Jews to pay reparations for the vessels of gold and silver which they had taken out of Egypt during the time of the Exodus a thousand years before (Exod 3:21-22).[7]

A port city was established in order to further Greek interests in Egypt and was named Alexandria after the new conqueror. This city was destined to develop into the largest commercial and cultural center of the eastern Mediterranean. A Greek culture which flourished there would dramatically affect the Diaspora Jews who, unlike their Judean brothers,

6. Victor Tcherikover believes that the Jews did meet with Alexander, but not in Jerusalem. The Talmud gives an account of the same story which is found in Josephus (*Antiquities* 11.8.3,5; cf. *Yoma* 69a). However, the Talmud places the meeting in Antipatris. This was a common rendezvous point between the Jews and anyone traversing the coastal plain. Tcherikover believes that Jerusalem was actually captured by Parmenio or some other Macedonian general while Alexander was laying siege to Tyre. He says, "Can it be assumed that the Jews did not make an effort to appear before Alexander, henceforth their king, when he passed through Palestine on his way to Egypt? Had they not done so they would have made themselves an exception among the peoples inhabiting Syria and Phoenicia, which would surely have provoked the just anger of the king. It can therefore be assumed that soon after the fall of Tyre the Jews sent representatives to welcome the king, and quite possibly waited to meet him at Kefar-Saba (Antipatris), the nearest to Jerusalem of all the places through which he passed" (Abraham Schalit, ed., *The Hellenistic Age*, The World History of the Jewish People, 6:61-62).
7. J. H. Hertz, ed., *The Pentateuch and Haftorahs*, p. 217.

readily assimilated the Hellenistic philosophy into their religion.[8]

After subduing Egypt, Alexander retraced his march north through Palestine, turning his conquest east into Babylon. Crossing the Tigris and the Euphrates, Alexander met the Persian army for the third time at Gaugamela. The year was 331 B.C. Again the Persian king, Darius III, fled the field of battle as he had done at Issus, and Alexander won a crowning victory over the armies which King Darius had abandoned. The Greeks pursued the fleeing Persian monarch toward the Caspian Sea. However, before they could overtake him, Darius was killed by his own officers. The struggle between Greece and Persia, whose roots reached back a century and a half to the time of Xerxes I, was then over. Alexander, assuming all of the trappings of an Oriental potentate, occupied the Persian king's chief cities of Babylon and Susa. So completely was Alexander captivated by Persian royalty that he donned Persian garb and enforced Persian protocol at court.

The next year, 330 B.C., Alexander continued his conquest, marching through Persia to Afghanistan. The limits of his march were reached in 326 B.C. when he invaded India. There his army refused to go further, and Alexander turned back, but not before he had conquered the world, for the borders of the Persian Empire represented the world as it was then known to the west.

---

8. Some rabbis say that the opposite is true. They maintain that the wisdom of the Greeks was not really Greek. The 14th-century physician, Meir Ben Isaac Aldabi, debated with some Gentiles who insisted that, because he was a Jew, he was incapable of grasping their philosophic arguments. However, Aldabi declared that these philosophic principles were actually derived from the Jews, for he had found in an ancient book this story: "Aristotle, whose system all the scholars follow and whose books they read, was the teacher of Alexander of Macedon who ruled the entire world. When Alexander conquered Jerusalem, he appointed Aristotle superintendent of King Solomon's archives, which had survived. Aristotle studied Solomon's manuscripts, translating them, made various additions, and gave them out as his own works; and in order that the truth not be known he hid the originals" (Israel Zinberg, *A History of Jewish Literature*, 3:161; Louis Ginzberg, *The Legends of the Jews*, 6:282-83.

Alexander the Great suddenly died in Babylon in 323 B.C. at the age of thirty-three. The great horn was broken (Dan 8:8).

THE WARS OF THE DIADOCHI

And when he shall stand up, his kingdom shall be broken, and shall be divided toward the four winds of heaven, but not to his posterity, nor according to his dominion wherewith he ruled; for his kingdom shall be plucked up, even for others besides these (Dan 11:4).

Fulfilled: 323-301 B.C.

Judea was an insignificant speck in the vast empire of Alexander the Great. In Europe his borders included Greece, Macedonia, and Thrace. From Asia Minor they ran south through Judea to Egypt. They included all of Syria. To this territory he added the regions which stretched along the Caspian Sea and the Indian Ocean as far east as the Indus River in India. Daniel said that Alexander, the "he-goat," would cover "the face of the whole earth" (Dan 8:5); and that he would "rule with great dominion" (11:3); and it came to pass just as Daniel had predicted 250 years before.

This was the first time in recorded history that so vast an empire had been assembled. And all of this territory was gathered beneath the scepter of Alexander within a dozen years. Daniel also observed this swift expansion of Alexander's conquest, saying that the ram moved so fast that his feet "touched not the ground" (8:5). A little more than a decade had elapsed between the time Alexander crossed the Hellespont at the age of twenty-three and that day in June 323 B.C. when he died—master of the world.

What Alexander had so quickly unified into one empire was dissolved over the next 200 years amid conflict led by the descendants of Alexander's top military leaders. However, the most intense part of this struggle was to occur within the next quarter century. This era is called "the period of the Diadochi," a Greek word meaning "successors." The successors included Antigonus I and his son Demetrius I, Antipater and his son Cassander, Seleucus, Ptolemy, Eumenes, and Lysimachus, all of whom fought over Alexander's empire after his death.

The period of the Diadochi is presented twice in the book of Daniel. It first occurs in Daniel 8:8 where the prophet says, "And the he-goat magnified himself exceedingly: and when he was strong, the great horn was broken; and instead of it there came up four notable horns toward the four winds of heaven."

The same vision occurs in our text. "And when he shall stand up, his kingdom shall be broken, and shall be divided toward the four winds of heaven, but not to his posterity, nor according to his dominion wherewith he ruled; for his kingdom shall be plucked up, even for others besides these" (11:4).

There were three possible heirs to Alexander's throne. First was a brother who was mentally deficient. Second, Alexander had a son who was born posthumously to Roxana, named Alexander. He was murdered in 311 b.c. Third was another son, Herakles, who was illegitimate, the child of Barsina, daughter of Darius III. None of these were serious contenders for the throne. Therefore Daniel said that his kingdom would be divided "not to his posterity."

After Alexander's death in 323 b.c. an attempt was made to preserve the unity of the empire. Perdiccas, a close friend of Alexander, was elected regent for all affairs of state while the generals became provincial satraps over different parts of the empire. This was contrary to Alexander's policy because it returned the administration of the empire back to the way things were in the Persian period under Darius III. It also gave the generals a strong base for future expansion.[9]

9. For a series of charts depicting the reduction of Alexander's reigning generals from 25 to 4, between 323 and 301 b.c., see Evelyn Shuckburgh, *The Histories of Polybius*, 2:560-61.

In 321 B.C. Perdiccas was assassinated by a group of conspirators after a reign of barely two years. After this, separate kingdoms emerged.

THE PTOLEMAIC KINGDOM IN EGYPT

One of the first generals to strive for the complete independence of his dominion was Ptolemy, governor of Egypt. He had a rich territory and was ready to go to war with anyone who challenged his complete authority. He extended his empire to include Cyrene in the west and Judea in the east. At Perdiccas's death, Ptolemy was picked to succeed him. However, Ptolemy, realizing how precarious this position was, refused. Content with his rule over Egypt, Ptolemy had the first province in the Alexandrian dominion which became an independent state. His kingdom, which started in 305 B.C., lasted longer than any of the other states which emerged out of Alexander's empire. Also the first of the Diadochi to rule over Judea, Ptolemy captured Jerusalem on a Sabbath when its inhabitants refused to fight.[10] This, by the way, would be a recurring problem in Jewish defences, solved only when Mattathias, during the Maccabean revolt a century and a half later, decreed that it was permissible to fight on the Sabbath.

THE SELEUCID KINGDOM IN SYRIA

With Ptolemy firmly established in Egypt, Seleucus, another rebel satrap, obtained Babylon in 321 B.C. when a second distribution of Alexander's empire occurred. Because his borders were less defensible than the borders of Ptolemy's Egypt, Seleucus had to struggle for his dominion often during the years of the Diadochi. His hold upon it was periodically lost, as for example, in 315 B.C. when he was forced to flee his

10. Josephus *Antiquities* 12.1.1; *Apion* 1.22; cf. Diodorus Siculus *Library of History* 18.43, who describes the war of 320 B.C. but does not mention this event.

kingdom and take refuge with Ptolemy when Antigonus attempted to add Seleucid's Babylonian regions to those already under his control. Three years later Seleucus, with the aid of Ptolemy, defeated Antigonus's son, Demetrius, at the Battle of Gaza and regained his lost territory. As a result of this battle, the foundation of the Seleucid Empire was firmly laid.

Incidentally, the date 312 b.c. is the accepted date for the beginning of the Seleucid kingdom. It is also used by Asiatic Greeks, as well as by the Jews, for dating documents. This chronology is found in First and Second Maccabees. The dates found in these two important sources can be converted to our reckoning by equating the year one of that era with the year 312 b.c.

The conflict between Seleucus and Antigonus continued for some years until Antigonus became convinced that he could not take Babylon from Seleucus. Antigonus was finally defeated in 310 b.c., and the Seleucid Empire then covered what was formerly the Persian Empire of Alexander.

Antigonus was the first of the Diadochi to call himself "king." He had ruled Phrygia in Asia Minor under Alexander. At the emperor's death, Antigonus, an old man then, along with his son, Demetrius, waged long and constant hostilities against Ptolemy, Seleucus, and others of Alexander's generals. They were finally defeated in 305 b.c. by Ptolemy. The Egyptian governor then called himself "king." This encouraged Seleucus, along with two other generals of Alexander, Lysimachus in Thrace and Cassander in Macedonia, to do the same. Therefore, 305 b.c. is the accepted date for the final demise of Alexander's empire. Then there were five kings ruling what Alexander had captured: Ptolemy, Seleucus, Lysimachus, Cassander, and Antigonus.

Antigonus made one final attempt to wrest the kingdom from his fellow generals. However, he was killed at the Battle of Ipsus in Asia Minor in 301 b.c.

THE FOUR WINDS

Alexander's kingdom "shall be divided toward the four winds of heaven," said the prophet. He used this figure, "the four winds,'" in each of the two visions which preview the rise of the Diadochi. It is a historical fact that only four of Alexander's generals finally emerged in control of his divided kingdom. However, it took nearly a quarter of a century after the king's death to determine just who the four would be. We now know that Ptolemy, Seleucus, Cassander, and Lysimachus finally emerged as "the four winds" in control of Alexander's empire.

Daniel's prophecy concerning "the four winds" was literally fulfilled in 301 B.C. Cassander ruled Macedonia, Lysimachus ruled Thrace and northern Asia Minor, Ptolemy ruled Egypt and Coele-Syria, while Seleucus ruled all the rest of Alexander's empire from Syria to Babylon. These are "the four winds" of Daniel 11:4 as well as the "four notable horns" of Daniel 8:8.

Cassander's kingdom was the first of the Hellenistic states to succumb to Rome. When he died in 293 B.C., his son was unable to retain the crown. It passed from hand to hand until the middle of the second century B.C. when the Romans took it.

Lysimachus was later killed in battle against Seleucus, who then added Thrace to his own huge kingdom. However, Seleucus himself was killed when he entered Macedonia to claim Lysimachus's domain.

Ptolemy lived to an advanced age. When he died in 285 B.C. he left a well-organized kingdom to his son Ptolemy II Philadelphus.

With the passing of the last of the Diadochi kings, a stormy era was terminated. This era witnessed the breakup of Alexander's empire, just as it was predicted by the prophet Daniel. The surviving Hellenistic states flourished for a time, only to be swallowed up by the Roman Empire in coming years.

The fate of the Palestinian Jews during the period of the Diadochi reflects the unsettled conditions of the empire itself. Judea changed rulers five times in twenty years. Each change was accompanied by great turmoil, loss of life, destruction of cities, and the deportation of some of its inhabitants. In 320 B.C. Ptolemy took Judea. In 315 B.C. it fell to Antigonus and then went back to Ptolemy in 312 B.C. However, Antigonus recaptured it in the same year and held it until 302 B.C. when Ptolemy captured it again. This is why Daniel observes this era in terms of four winds sweeping across the landscape. Tcherikover says,

> The period of the Diadochi . . . introduced new political principles into the life of the ancient world, the main motive factor being the unrestricted strength of a forceful personality aspiring for power. The Macedonian people produced within a brief space a large number of aggressive characters, who used the confusion of the period to make themselves absolute rulers.[11]

THE ENDURING INFLUENCE OF ALEXANDER'S CONQUEST

Some of the rabbis taught that Alexander the Great would be the last world ruler to precede the Kingdom of the Messiah. The Midrash of Rabbi Eliezer says,

> The (last human) king was Alexander of Macedonia, who ruled from one end of the world to the other, as it is said, "And as I was considering, behold, an he-goat came from the west over the face of the *whole* earth" (Dan. 8:5). "Over the earth" is not written here, but "over the whole earth." . . . The (ultimate) king is King Messiah, who, in the future, will rule from one end of the world to the other, as it is said, ". . . . and the stone that smote the image became a great mountain, and filled *the whole earth*."[12]

In its influence, the kingdom of Alexander did remain

---

11. Victor Tcherikover, *Hellenistic Civilization of the Jews*, p. 9.
12. Gerald Friedlander, *Pirkê De Rabbi Eliezer*, pp. 82-83.

longer than any of the others. Rome's imperial might ultimately swallowed up the Greek states of Alexander. Nevertheless, Hellenism conquered Rome. And it continues to conquer, as long as our civilization prevails, for today's Western culture is derived largely from the Hellenism of the Greeks.

The prophetic Scriptures present Alexander the Great as a mighty world conqueror. It is generally conceded that this conquest was one of military power, and so it was. However, Alexander invaded the east with something besides military might, for he also brought with him a body of ideas. This Greek way of looking at life was to mix their way of life with Oriental customs and form the Hellenistic culture which changed the face of the east.

These ideas were the result of the mental activity of the Greek people who called themselves Hellenes. Their concepts were embodied in the language they spoke, the literature they wrote, the art which they produced, the philosophy which they constructed, and the political structures which they developed. Generally, Hellenistic culture was a unique way of looking at the world and of reacting to it, which was embodied in Greek literature, art, science, politics, and religion.

In 2 Maccabees 4:13, "Hellenism" means the adoption of Greek customs. During the Hellenistic period, from the conquests of Alexander (336-323 B.C.) to the reign of the Roman emperor Augustus (27 B.C.–A.D. 14), Greek culture substituted cosmopolitan trends for eastern provincialism. The harmony and natural beauty of individualism were extolled in all forms of cultural expression. While Hellenism did not affect the masses until the Roman period, it flourished among the upper classes, especially in western Asia's new cities.

Alexander had been educated in the best of these Hellenistic traditions, for Aristotle himself was his private teacher. Alexander's world view was thoroughly hellenized. Consequently, he not only imposed the might of the Greek armies upon the east, but he also introduced these unique Greek ideas about the world upon his conquered countries. He opened the door for the influx of Hellenistic culture which would have far-reaching effects upon the east in general and disastrous effects upon the Jews in particular, though the traumatic consequences of the Hellenistic invasion of Judea did not climax until a century and a half later. Alexander's introduction of Hellenism into the ancient world during the fourth century B.C. had far-reaching effects in unifying the east. Nevertheless, this Hellenism, with its refined polytheistic depravity, and Judaism, with its ethical monotheism, were destined to come into head-on conflict.

The crisis came during the reign of Antiochus IV Epiphanes in the second century B.C.

When the conquests of Alexander the Great introduced the Greek way into the eastern world, there was no attempt at first to force Hellenism upon the Jews. Its subtle influence did make considerable inroads long before the crisis broke during the reign of King Antiochus. This was especially true in the urban areas and among the Diaspora. The Jews of Alexandria, for example, had given up the sacred Hebrew and Aramaic vernacular as early as the reign of Ptolemy II Philadelpus (285-247 B.C.). So thorough was their hellenization that the leaders of the Jewish community recognized the need for the Torah in Greek. The result was the Septuagint.

Alexander the Great represents the watershed of those influences which were destined throughout their history to influence the Jews.

During the first millennium of their history, the destiny of the Hebrew people, as far as outside pressures were concerned, came entirely from the east. But, during the second millennium of Jewish history, beginning in the fourth century B.C., the west became the intellectual milieu in which the Jews had to struggle to retain their spiritual and cultural uniqueness. Following the Greek kingdoms of the Ptolemies and the

Seleucids came Rome. The Jews were first *drawn* into the Roman Empire; then they were crushed by it when they attempted to revolt against its imperial might. This hegemony of Greece and Rome in Judea lasted for almost a thousand years, from the advent of Alexander the Great in the fourth century B.C., until the fifth century A.D. when the Roman Empire began to fall apart. During this time the Jews' spiritual uniqueness was constantly threatened by Hellenism, Judaism's most subtle adversary.

The presence of Hellenism remained a constant threat because of a unique enticement, the Greek language. Koine, or common Greek, continually exposed the Jewish experience to the viable concepts of Hellenism. This alien culture struck roots in Judea with the spread of this beautifully articulate language. As Alexander's Greek mercenaries moved across the eastern world, so did the Greek idiom in which they spoke. It was destined to become the lingua franca of the Graeco-Roman world. But it also was destined to open the door to all that had been written by the Greeks concerning science, religion, philosophy, politics, and the arts. Of course, this meant that the New Testament would be written in Greek instead of the Aramaic vernacular or the Hebrew of the Old Testament. It is true that the Greek language proved the perfect medium for the revelation of Christian doctrine. Nevertheless, it was a curse to the Jews, for Greek formed the channel down which the pagan influence of Hellenism flowed during the interbiblical period into the Holy Land. So hated was this medium of Hellenism that the rabbis of the Talmudic era contemptuously refused to learn Greek.

During the summer of 1964, John Cullinane, an American archaeologist from Chicago, excavated the fictional tell at Makor. A workman, finding a fragment of a Greek statue, brought it to him. It is a marble hand grasping a stirgil. This statue, if it were ever found, says novelist James Michener in *The Source,* would epitomize the long struggle which stubborn Jews had conducted to protect their austere monotheism against the allurements of Greece. The statue of the Greek athlete had no doubt once adorned a gymnasium at Makor, the pagan center from which Greek officials had tried to impress their will on subject Jews, and as Cullinane sketched the find he could hear the sophisticated philosophers from Athens arguing with the awkward Jews: he could hear the tempting rationalizations of those who followed Zeus and Aphrodite as they clashed against the immovable monotheism of the Jews; and he could visualize the struggle in which Hellenism, one of the most spontaneous civilizations in history, had tried to smother Judaism, one of the most rigid.[13]

The conflict between Hellenism and Judaism was to heat up during the next century or so after the Diadochi. While the pressure of Hellenism remained constant upon the Jews, the political circumstances of the land altered from time to time. The descendants of Ptolemy and Seleucus contended for control of Coele-Syria all during the third century B.C. However, the Ptolemies of Egypt dominated the land of Israel most of this time. Then, in the early second century B.C., Antiochus III the Great of Syria wrested the land from its Ptolemaic rulers. It was during the ensuing years of the Seleucid overlords that the Jews were to suffer most from the intensifying threat of Hellenism. Finally, during the reign of Antiochus IV Epiphanes, the Jews were to be persecuted and physically coerced into yielding to this Greek way of life. This resistance issued in the Maccabean revolt. The tides turned and Judaism prevailed, though Hellenism still remains a subtle threat to Judaism even to this day.

13. James A. Michener, *The Source*, p. 58.

2

The Struggle Between Ptolemies and Seleucids

Daniel 11:5-20

Fulfilled: 300-175 B.C.

DURING THE THIRD CENTURY B.C. there was a constant struggle between Egypt's house of Ptolemy and Syria's house of Seleucus. Daniel 11:5-20 is a record of this struggle.

Sandwiched in between the two kingdoms of Egypt and Syria lay Israel, "like to a ship in a storm which is tossed by the waves on both sides," observes Josephus.[1] Israel was the buffer state between these two great contesting powers. This little narrow land bridge connecting Europe, Africa, and Asia became a "focus of forces," to use novelist James Michener's terminology,[2] for the armies of the Ptolemies and the Seleucids marched back and forth across Israel during this century.

The events of Daniel 11:5-20 cover these 125 years of Jewish history, running between 300 and 175 B.C., and have to do with the Jews' two antagonists, Egypt and Syria. Their object was the control of Coele-Syria, of which Judea was a part. During this entire era, the king of the south, Ptolemy I Soter of Egypt, and his descendants would vie with the king of the north, Seleucus I Nicator, the king of Syria, and his descendants for control of the glorious land, Israel.

To understand these verses, a historical review of this third-century struggle between the Ptolemies and the Seleucids is necessary. Egypt is mentioned by name in verse 8. Syria is

1. Josephus *Antiquities* 12.3.3.
2. James A. Michener, *The Source*, p. 150.

not. The reason is that Egypt in the third century B.C. covered essentially the same geographical territory as it did during the time of Daniel in the sixth century B.C. However, the Syrian empire of Seleucus was not known in Daniel's day. Persia was then the ascending world power in the east. Thus, Egypt is mentioned by name while Syria is not.

The prophet Daniel is much like the Greek historian Polybius, who was taken as a captive to Rome in 166 B.C. There he conceived the idea of writing his histories in order to explain how the entire world, in only a few years, fell under the control of a single country, Rome.[3] Daniel is the Jewish counterpart of Polybius, for his purpose was somewhat the same. However, Daniel's scope is far broader, for in chapter 11 the prophet's vision sweeps from his day into the distant future, where he sees the whole world brought under the sway of a climactic Gentile world power, the universal kingdom of the Antichrist.

In one segment of his great vision, that which presents the third-century B.C. struggle between the Ptolemies and the Seleucids (11:5-20), Daniel anticipates in prophecy what Polybius would later record as history. Consequently, reference must be continually made to Polybius, along with other primary sources, for historical verification of this portion of Daniel's vision.

Though they were written nearly three centuries before the actual events took place, these prophecies in Daniel 11 are so historically accurate that many scholars refuse to acknowledge a sixth-century B.C. date for them. Rather, these modern critics hold that the scroll of Daniel was written during the Maccabean era and that these prophecies are actually a historic review in prophetic guise of events which already have taken

---

3. Polybius *Histories* 1.1; see also F. W. Walbank, *A Historical Commentary on Polybius*, p. 40, for other references to this theme. Cf. James A. Montgomery, *A Critical and Exegetical Commentary on the Book of Daniel*, p. 421.

place. Nothing is new about this theory. It was advanced very early by the pagan philosopher Porphyry.[4]

It is true that we are now reading history in much of Daniel 11. However, when these predictions were made by the prophet in the sixth century B.C., all was in the future. Yet, prophecy is history—history written in advance. And this history is "His-Story," as Dr. Ironside used to say. Therefore, we have no a priori assumptions about Daniel 11 which would preclude the miracle of forecasting the future precisely and accurately under the inspiration of the Holy Spirit. Daniel 11 is either a pious fraud, as some scholars say, or an example of the absolute, unerring precision of God's holy Word.

We choose the latter.

Our position is that Daniel was an actual person who lived in Babylon in the sixth century B.C. during the Exile. The events which happened in Daniel have historical validity. His visions, which also came during the sixth century B.C., are predictive in nature. The literal fulfillment of these prophecies began immediately, even in Daniel's day, with the fall of Babylon. Their fulfillment continued through the great Gentile empires of Persia, Greece, and Rome. Therefore, much of what Daniel predicted has already found literal fulfillment— but not all. A prophetic precedent has been set and verified in the concourse of history, as we shall see. Therefore, some of Daniel's material which has not as yet found fulfillment will be literally fulfilled in the end days.

The king of the north and the king of the south, Seleucus

4. Gleason L. Archer, trans., *Jerome's Commentary on Daniel*, p. 15, reads, "Porphyry wrote his twelfth book against the prophecy of Daniel, denying that it was composed by the person to whom it is ascribed in its title, but rather by some individual living in Judaea at the time of Antiochus who was surnamed Epiphanes. He furthermore alleged that 'Daniel' did not foretell the future so much as he related the past, and lastly that whatever he spoke of up till the time of Antiochus contained authentic history, whereas anything he may have conjectured beyond that point was false, inasmuch as he would not have foreknown the future." For a defense of the 6th-century B.C. apocalypses of Daniel, see Robert Dick Wilson, *Studies in the Book of Daniel*, 2:101-16.

and Ptolemy, are so designated because their countries border Judea on the north and south. The kingdoms of the other two Diadochi, Cassander and Lysimachus, drop from view, for they have nothing further to do with Israel's destiny. It is a basic principle of biblical interpretation that the prophetic Word includes only those countries which in some way affect Israel, the covenant people of God.

In addition, Daniel 11 presents a view of Gentile world rule in a studied pattern. The prophet moves deductively, narrowing his field, as he proceeds in his prophetic vision forward through the centuries.

He begins with the Persian rulers of the fifth century B.C. (Dan 11:2). He then views the rise of Alexander the Great and the Hellenistic world supremacy of the fourth century B.C. (11:3). Then, as if he had reached a meridian, Daniel's vision begins to narrow. From among the empires of the Diadochi (11:4), he deletes two and focuses upon the remaining estates of Ptolemy in Egypt and Seleucus in Syria (11:5-20). Finally, Egypt is eliminated and successive kings of Syria are paraded before us until we come to the evil acme of Gentile sway, the reign of Antiochus IV Epiphanes (11:21-34).

Daniel does not, at this time, move on to preview the fourth world empire, Rome, as he does in chapters 2 and 7, for he has found the counterpart of the Antichrist in the person of King Antiochus. Daniel traces successive Gentile rulers down to Antiochus Epiphanes and there stops, for the person of King Antiochus dramatically portrays the final world ruler.

We conclude that Daniel's purpose in chapter 11 is to carry his revelation forward from the Persian rulers of his day, through the Greek Ptolemaic and Seleucid orbits, until he comes to Antiochus IV Epiphanes. Then, at that point in history, his vision leaps out into the distant future where he presents the final Gentile world ruler, the Antichrist, who will usurp universal jurisdiction just before the Messiah ushers in the ultimate world order of righteousness.

The transition point from the near future to the far distant future comes when Daniel views the Seleucid king, Antiochus Epiphanes. Seeing that he and his era duplicate, in microcosm, what will occur in the reign of the Antichrist during the Great Tribulation in the end days, Daniel typifies the Antichrist and the Great Tribulation period through the person and reign of King Antiochus.

It is in the first twenty verses of Daniel 11 that the prophet sets the stage for the entrance of Antiochus IV Epiphanes, history's great type of the Antichrist. Therefore, Daniel 11:5-20 contains historical narrative which is unparalleled in the prophetic Word. Historical facts accumulate rapidly as Daniel's vision moves from one Ptolemaic and Seleucid king to another. Not all of the kings who reigned in Egypt and Syria during the third century B.C. are mentioned. The prophet considers only those kings, battles, and political intrigues which advance the story of Gentile dominion from the first Seleucus to Antiochus IV.

We have discussed the breakup of Alexander's empire following his death in 323 B.C. and the rise of the Diadochi. Their struggle for lands extended to the end of the fourth century when Ptolemy and Seleucus emerged as the rulers of Egypt and Syria, respectively. The Ptolemies were in control of Coele-Syria, where Judea was located, from the time of the Battle of Ipsus, 301 B.C., forward. However, the sons of Seleucus were never to rest until this province became theirs. Seleucus II Callinicus attempted to drive out the Egyptian rule but was unsuccessful.

It was not until the accession of King Antiochus III the Great to the Seleucid throne many years later that the ejection of the Ptolemaic rule in Coele-Syria was realized. Antiochus the Great failed at first when he was defeated by Ptolemy IV Philopator at the Battle of Raphia in 217 B.C. However, when Ptolemy Philopator died, his four-year-old son followed him upon the throne. Egypt was weakened by the political intrigue which attended the regency of the young pharaoh, Ptolemy V Epiphanes. This gave Antiochus the Great the chance that he wanted, and by 198 B.C. Coele-Syria was firmly in his control. The Ptolemies would never rule there again. Thus, after more than a century, the great-great-grandson of the first Seleucus wrested Judea from the great-great-grandson of the first Ptolemy.

Daniel 11:5-20 is the story of that struggle. Israel is the arena where these two superpowers clashed.

Attempts to expound Daniel 11:5-20 have been notoriously tedious. A confounding array of unfamiliar names, dates, battles, and political intrigues challenge every endeavor to relate Daniel's prophecy to its fulfillment in the historical events of the third century B.C. To explain every detail would reproduce what Mahaffy and Bevan have done.[5] However, to make only passing reference to these events would tend to blunt the marvelous precision of Daniel's forecast.

In spite of their tedium, the effort to relate these verses to their historical fulfillment is rewarding for they remind us how accurately the Word of God, given under the inspiration of the Holy Spirit, can declare the future.

THE KING OF THE SOUTH: PTOLEMY I SOTER OF EGYPT

THE KING OF THE NORTH: SELEUCUS I NICATOR OF SYRIA

> And the king of the south shall be strong, and one of his princes: and he shall be strong above him, and have dominion; his dominion shall be a great dominion (Dan 11:5).

Fulfilled: 321-280 B.C.

Daniel begins his detailed prediction about the political events of the third century B.C. between Egypt and Syria by observing the relative strength of the king of the south and the king of the north. The issue is not whether this house or that

---

5. J. P. Mahaffy, *The Empire of the Ptolemies;* Edwyn R. Bevan, *The House of Seleucus,* 2 vols.

house prevails in battle, for all during the third century B.C. the Ptolemies would be the stronger of the two houses. Rather, their relative importance is measured by the extent of their jurisdiction.

"The king of the south" is Alexander's general, Ptolemy I Soter, who ruled Egypt between 321 and 285 B.C. He took the title *king* in 305 B.C. "The south," Hebrew *negeb,* usually refers to that territory which lies in the southern part of Judea. However, in Daniel 11 it regularly denotes Egypt.

But who is "one of his princes" who is introduced in this verse and who "shall be strong above him"? It is generally agreed that this prince is the Diadochi, Seleucus I Nicator, who became one of Ptolemy's generals when he was forced to flee Antigonus in 315 B.C. He took refuge in Egypt, where Ptolemy Soter made him a general. While in command of the Egyptian army, he defeated Antigonus at the Battle of Gaza in 321 B.C. As a result, Seleucus Nicator recovered his Babylonian satrapy. Therefore, October 1, 312 B.C. is the date for the beginning of the Seleucid era. All historical events were later dated by this episode according to Jewish reckoning.[6]

From the Egyptian point of view, Seleucus I Nicator was indeed "one of his [Ptolemy's] princes." After a crowning victory over Antigonus at Ipsus in 301 B.C. in which he regained all his lost territories, Seleucus Nicator's borders stretched from Asia Minor to India, excepting Coele-Syria which remained under the Ptolemies. He also founded a new capital at Antioch on the Orontes River in 300 B.C. Seleucus Nicator's dominion was, in fact, greater than Ptolemy's for it was by far the largest of those carved out of the empire of Alexander the Great. King Seleucus I was "the most regal and ruler of the greatest extent of territory after Alexander," says Aarian.[7] He is the true heir of Alexander, and therefore Daniel focuses

6. Cf. 1 Macc 1:10; Josephus *Antiquities* 13.6.7.
7. Flavius Aarian *Anabasis of Alexander* 7.2.

upon him and his descendants, while finally dropping the Ptolemies from his vision.

The century-long rule of Egypt over Coele-Syria began in 301 B.C. when Ptolemy I Soter captured this territory for the fourth time. Though the Ptolemies were to fight five wars with the Seleucids during the third century B.C. in order to keep it, they would retain control over Judea for most of this century. This era represents almost a total blank in the pages of recorded Jewish history. It is fortunate that some of the important political events of those days are reflected in Daniel 11:5-20.

Besides Egypt, the Ptolemaic rule over Coele-Syria extended north to Phoenicia, then across to Damascus and, from thence, out into the desert. All of Transjordan, as far as the desert, represented the eastern frontier of the Ptolemaic dominion in the land. With only short intervals, Judea would remain in the hands of the Ptolemies up until 198 B.C. Then it moved into the Seleucid orbit until the Hasmonean kings of Judea established themselves, only to be relieved of their province by the Romans around 64-63 B.C.

THE KING OF THE SOUTH: PTOLEMY II PHILADELPHUS
THE KING OF THE NORTH: ANTIOCHUS II THEOS

> And at the end of years they shall join themselves together; and the daughter of the king of the south shall come to the king of the north to make an agreement: but she shall not retain the strength of her arm; neither shall he stand, nor his arm; but she shall be given up, and they that brought her, and he that begat her, and he that strengthened her in those times (Dan 11:6).

Fulfilled: 249-246 B.C.

"And at the end of years," that is, after some years, "they shall join themselves together; and the daughter of the king of the south shall come to the king of the north to make an agreement."

Thirty-one years, 280 until 249 B.C., elapse between verses 5 and 6. Weary for the moment of the hostilities between the two houses, Ptolemy II Philadelphus gave his daughter, Berenice, in marriage to the Seleucid king, Antiochus II Theos. A large dowry went with Berenice. Antiochus Theos, in turn, agreed to divorce his present wife, Laodice, and to cut off his two sons from inheriting the throne in deference to any son which might be born of his union with Berenice.

Berenice was brought to Antioch, the Syrian capital, with great pomp. Her father, Ptolemy II Philadelphus, accompanied the entourage as far as Pelusium, apparently to guarantee the safety of the impressive dowry amounting "to countless thousands of gold and silver," according to the calculations of Jerome.[8] It was so impressive that the people called Ptolemy Philadelphus by the nickname "Phernophoros" or "Dowrygiver."

However, this strategy failed to keep the peace. The rest of verse 6 indicates the following events: A son was born of Antiochus II Theos and Berenice. But within two years, Berenice's father, the king of Egypt, died. Antiochus Theos then divorced Berenice, having become reconciled with his first wife, Laodice. However, fearing her husband's fickleness, Laodice poisoned him.[9] She also had Berenice and her child murdered, along with those who had accompanied the Egyptian queen to the court of Antioch. All of this was predicted by Daniel in precise detail:

> But she [Berenice] shall not retain the strength of her arm [she is divorced by Antiochus Theos]; neither shall he stand [Antiochus Theos is poisoned], nor his arm [his son by Berenice is also murdered]; but she shall be given up [Berenice is put to death at the instigation of Laodice], and they that brought her [Berenice's Egyptian entourage is also slain], and he that begat her [Berenice's father, Ptolemy

8. Archer, p. 122.
9. Ibid.; Appian *The Syrian Wars* 65.

Philadelphus, died in 246 B.C.], and he that strengthened her in those times [presumably her husband, Antiochus Theos, who also died in 246 B.C.] (Dan 11:6).

THE KING OF THE SOUTH: PTOLEMY III EUERGETES
THE KING OF THE NORTH: SELEUCUS II CALLINICUS

But out of a shoot from her roots shall one stand up in his place, who shall come unto the army, and shall enter into the fortress of the king of the north, and shall deal against them, and shall prevail: and also their gods, with their molten images, and with their goodly vessels of silver and of gold, shall he carry captive into Egypt; and he shall refrain some years from the king of the north. And he shall come into the realm of the king of the south, but he shall return unto his own land (Dan 11:7-9).

Fulfilled: 246-240 B.C.

Daniel's vision moves into the next generation and focuses upon Ptolemy III Euergetes and his Syrian rival, Seleucus II Callinicus.

"But out of a shoot from her roots shall one stand up in his place." Berenice's brother, Ptolemy III Euergetes, followed their father on the throne of Egypt. He was called "Euergetes," meaning "Benefactor," by the Egyptians because he recaptured some gods which Cambyses had taken from Egypt 280 years before. He invaded Syria "to revenge the murder of Berenice," affirms Polybius.[10] Daniel said he "shall come unto the army, and shall enter into the fortress of the king of the north, and shall deal against them, and shall prevail: and also their gods, with their molten images, and with their goodly vessels of silver and of gold, shall he carry captive into Egypt."

This prophecy has several details. First, he "shall enter into the fortress of the king of the north." It is generally agreed that Ptolemy II Euergetes captured Seleucia, the fortified port

10. Polybius, 5.58.

of Antioch in Syria (cf. Acts 13:1, 4). He carried off booty amounting to 40,000 talents of silver, plus 2,500 precious vessels and images of their gods.[11] Soon Ptolemy Euergetes was called home because of an insurrection which had broken out there. On his way he stopped off in Jerusalem to offer a thank offering to the God of the Jews for his victory, according to Josephus.[12]

At this point in history, Ptolemy III Euergetes could have captured the whole of Syria, for "there was much confusion in the house of Seleucidae," says Appian.[13] The rebellion in Egypt diverted his attention from conquest to the home front. Capitalizing upon Ptolemy's problems at home, Seleucus II Callinicus invaded Egypt. Daniel says, "He shall come into the realm of the king of the south." However, the armies of Ptolemy Euergetes defeated Seleucus Callinicus so badly that the prophecy that he "shall return to his own land" was fulfilled. Only a remnant of his forces was left intact.

The year was 240 B.C., the only time that Ptolemaic rule in Coele-Syria was seriously threatened during all of that century.

THE KING OF THE SOUTH: PTOLEMY IV PHILOPATOR AND
PTOLEMY V EPIPHANES

THE KING OF THE NORTH: SELEUCUS III CERAUNUS AND
ANTIOCHUS III THE GREAT

And his sons shall war, and shall assemble a multitude of great forces, which shall come on, and overflow, and pass through; and they shall return and war, even to his fortress. And the king of the south shall be moved with anger, and shall come forth and fight with him, even with the king of the north; and he shall set forth a great multitude, and the multitude shall be given into his hand. And the multitude shall be lifted up, and his heart shall be exalted; and he shall cast down tens of thousands, but he

11. Archer, p. 123.
12. Josephus *Apion* 2.5.
13. Appian, 65.

shall not prevail. And the king of the north shall return, and shall set forth a multitude greater than the former; and he shall come on at the end of the times, even of years, with a great army and with much substance. And in those times there shall many stand up against the king of the south: also the children of the violent among thy people shall lift themselves up to establish the vision; but they shall fall. So the king of the north shall come, and cast up a mound, and take a well-fortified city: and the forces of the south shall not stand, neither his chosen people, neither shall there be any strength to stand. But he that cometh against him shall do according to his own will, and none shall stand before him; and he shall stand in the glorious land, and in his hand shall be destruction. And he shall set his face to come with the strength of his whole kingdom, and with him equitable conditions; and he shall perform them: and he shall give him the daughter of women, to corrupt her; but she shall not stand, neither be for him. After this shall he turn his face unto the isles, and shall take many: but a prince shall cause the reproach offered by him to cease; yea, moreover, he shall cause his reproach to turn upon him. Then he shall turn his face toward the fortresses of his own land; but he shall stumble and fall, and shall not be found (Dan 11:10-19).

Fulfilled: 226-187 B.C.

"His sons" (11:10), that is, the sons of Seleucus II Callinicus, now come into Daniel's view. They were Seleucus III Ceraunus and Antiochus III the Great. The former had reigned only two years before he was murdered. He was followed upon the throne of Syria by his illustrious brother, Antiochus the Great, who was destined to raise the Seleucid Empire to its greatest glory until it clashed head on with the rising Roman Empire, where Antiochus the Great was summarily eclipsed.

These two brothers, Seleucus III Ceraunus, followed by Antiochus III the Great, "shall war, and shall assemble a multitude of great forces, which shall come on, and overflow, and pass through; and they shall return and war, even to his fortress" (11:10). The plural is used in this verse because Seleucus Ceraunus led the campaign until he was killed in Asia Minor. Antiochus III the Great then took over the operation, resuming the war with Ptolemy IV Philopator in 219 B.C. His campaigns in Syria in 219 B.C. and in Coele-Syria in 218 B.C. are described by Daniel in terms of "great forces, which shall come on, and overflow, and pass through."

"And they shall return and war, even to his fortress" suggests that Antiochus III the Great in the spring of 217 B.C., after wintering in Ptolemais, renewed the attack upon Egypt. That time he moved south to "his fortress," in other words to Ptolemy's fortress at Gaza or Raphia. The proximity of the Syrian army angered Ptolemy IV Philopator, who marched his armies up from Alexandria to engage Antiochus the Great. "And the king of the south shall be moved with anger, and shall come forth and fight with him, even with the king of the north; and he shall set forth a great multitude, and the multitude shall be given into his hand" (11:11). His casualties amounted to 10,000 infantry, 300 cavalry, 6 elephants, besides 4,000 men taken prisoner, according to Polybius.[14]

Antiochus III the Great fell back to Gaza and then retreated to Antioch. However, Ptolemy IV Philopator did not prevail, for he failed to follow up his victory. He was an effeminate and dissolute character who did not have the energy to complete the overthrow of King Antiochus.[15] Ptolemy Philopator died a dozen years after the Battle of Raphia. His four-year-old son, Ptolemy V Epiphanes, succeeded him on the throne.

During the dozen years which passed after the Battle of Raphia there was virtual peace between Egypt and Syria. Antiochus III the Great was busy in the eastern part of his

14. Polybius, 5.86.
15. R. H. Charles, *A Critical and Exegetical Commentary on the Book of Daniel*, pp. 286-87.

empire where he succeeded in establishing himself in Persia, Bactria, and India. He returned to the stage of Daniel's prophecy "at the end of the times, even of years" (11:13b). His success in the east also enabled him to gather a large army. "And the king of the north shall return, and shall set forth a multitude greater than the former" (11:13). Antiochus the Great renewed his fight with Egypt with an even larger army than the one which Ptolemy IV Philopator routed at the Battle of Raphia. Antiochus was joined by Philip, king of Macedonia, in an alliance against Egypt. There was also a revolt in Egypt, according to Jerome.[16] Thus Daniel said, "And in those times there shall many stand up against the king of the south" (11:14).

In addition, some Jews also joined this rebellion, for it was revealed to Daniel that "the children of the violent among thy people shall lift themselves up to establish the vision; but they shall fall" (11:14). The identity of these Jews is unknown. Apparently they were acting according to some prophecy which they expected to be fulfilled in the overthrow of Egypt. However, whatever they expected to accomplish failed.

The Egyptian general, Scopas, was sent by Ptolemy V Epiphanes into Syria in 198 B.C. to try to regain territory which had been lost. However, Antiochus III the Great defeated the Egyptian general, and Scopas was forced to flee to the fortified city of Sidon for refuge. There he was shut up with 10,000 men. Attempts were made by three of Egypt's best military men to rescue Scopas and his troops. However, "the forces of the south shall not stand, neither his chosen people, neither shall there be any strength to stand" (11:15). King Antiochus, surrounding the city, threw up earthworks, and the city was captured, as was foretold: "So the king of the north shall come, and cast up a mound, and take a well-fortified city" (11:15).

Ptolemaic rule in Coele-Syria was then permanently lost,

16. Archer, p. 125.

and Antiochus III the Great was in firm control of Israel, "the glorious land" (11:16).

The Seleucids would hold the land from this time forward, though their rule was weakened by the Maccabean revolt. Nevertheless, they would retain control after 165 B.C., but their dominion diminished, tentatively yielding to the Hasmonean dynasty of Jewish kings, and then finally to the Romans.

At this point in his career, Antiochus III the Great was determined to overthrow Ptolemy V Epiphanes. "And he shall set his face to come with the strength of his whole kingdom" (11:17) is Daniel's metaphor indicating this determination. But it was never carried out. Before the invasion could take place, Antiochus the Great came to terms with Egypt. Presenting what Ptolemy Epiphanes thought were "equitable conditions," King Antiochus betrothed his daughter, Cleopatra, to the Egyptian king. Antiochus intended to "corrupt her," for his strategy was to use his daughter to gain Egypt. "But she shall not stand, neither be for him" (11:17). Cleopatra proved to be more faithful to her Egyptian husband than loyal to her father, and his plans for gaining control of Egypt through her failed.

Finally, Daniel 11:18-19 predicted the Waterloo of Antiochus III the Great. "After this shall he turn his face unto the isles, and shall take many" (11:18). In 196 B.C. he captured most of Asia Minor. In the same year Antiochus the Great crossed the Hellespont. Taking time out to consolidate his conquests, he then invaded Greece in 192 B.C. and established himself north of Corinth. There his conquests came to an end.

In 191 B.C. his forces were defeated by the Romans at Thermopylae. He retreated to Ephesus. But by then the Romans were determined to expel Antiochus III the Great from Asia. They sent General Lucius Cornelius Scipio against him the following year. At the Battle of Magnesia near Smyrna in the autumn of 190 B.C., Antiochus's huge army of 80,000 was defeated with great losses. Scipio, "the prince" whom Daniel saw, "shall cause the reproach offered by him to cease; yea, moreover, he shall cause his reproach to turn upon him" (11: 18). As a result of his defeat, Antiochus the Great gave up all claim to Europe and western Asia Minor. Livy reveals the humiliating terms of settlement imposed upon him by the Romans.[17] Besides the territory which he was to concede to Rome, he was to pay 15,000 talents, a staggering amount of money. Five hundred talents were to be paid immediately, 2,500 more when the Roman Senate ratified the peace terms, and then 1,000 annually for the next 12 years. In addition, Antiochus the Great was to deliver 20 hostages to Rome to guarantee the peace. Hannibal, whom Antiochus had befriended, was to be surrendered also, along with some other men wanted by the conquerors for plotting war against Rome. Among the 20 hostages to go to Rome was the Syrian king's son, Antiochus IV Epiphanes.

In order to pay this heavy reparation laid upon him by the Romans, Antiochus III the Great turned "his face toward the fortresses of his own land." He was slain while plundering a wealthy temple in Elymais. In prophetic vision, Daniel witnessed this event, recording that Antiochus the Great "shall stumble and fall, and shall not be found" (11:19).

THE KING OF THE NORTH: SELEUCUS IV PHILOPATOR

Then shall stand up in his place one that shall cause an exactor to pass through the glory of the kingdom; but within few days he shall be destroyed, neither in anger, nor in battle (Dan 11:20).

Fulfilled: 187-175 B.C.

Antiochus III the Great left two sons, Seleucus IV Philopator and Antiochus IV Epiphanes, both of whom followed him

17. Livy *The History of Rome* 37.45.

upon the throne. Daniel 11:20 presents the first of these two sons, Seleucus Philopator, to "stand up in his place."

The one thing that Daniel noted about the reign of Seleucus IV Philopator, besides his murder, was that he would cause "an exactor to pass through the glory of the kingdom." At this point Daniel seemed to ignore international intrigues and to focus exclusively upon the relationship between Judea and her Syrian overlords.

Again Daniel's deductive method is apparent. Beginning with the great world empires of Persia and Greece in the fifth and fourth centuries B.C., Daniel narrowed his vision to the provincial struggle between Egypt and Syria over Coele-Syria. Then, finally he focused upon Judea itself, and particularly upon Jerusalem.

But we shall also note that while Daniel focuses downward from the world conquests of Alexander the Great to the provincial persecutions of Antiochus IV Epiphanes in Judea, at this point his field of vision again widens. Its scope comprehends in prophetic medium the world orbit of the Antichrist, followed by the Messiah's universal dominion.

Second Maccabees 3 records the story of "the exactor" whom Seleucus IV Philopator sent to Jerusalem.

There was one Simon, a Benjaminite and a guardian of the Temple, who had a falling out with Onias III, the high priest. This Simon told Apollonius, governor of Syria, about the great treasure stored in the Temple. Apollonius related the story to the king, Seleucus IV Philopator, who, still laboring to pay the heavy war reparations laid upon his father by Rome, sent Heliodorus, "the exactor," to Jerusalem to seize this treasure. When it was learned what Heliodorus was about to do, the entire city lamented this sacrilege. As the people prostrated themselves and prayed, Heliodorus, the king's emissary, entered the sacred precincts of the Temple. Then it happened:

But at the very moment when he arrived with his bodyguard

at the treasury, the Ruler of spirits and of all powers produced a mighty apparition, so that all who had the audacity to accompany Heliodorus were faint with terror, stricken with panic at the power of God. They saw a horse, splendidly caparisoned, with a rider of terrible aspect; it rushed fiercely at Heliodorus and, rearing up, attacked him with its hooves. The rider was wearing golden armour. There also appeared to Heliodorous two young men of surpassing strength and glorious beauty, splendidly dressed. They stood on either side of him and scourged him, raining ceaseless blows upon him. He fell suddenly to the ground, overwhelmed by a great darkness, and his men snatched him up and put him on a litter. This man, who so recently had entered the treasury with a great throng and his whole bodyguard, was now borne off by them quite helpless, publicly compelled to acknowledge the sovereignty of God (2 Macc 3:24-28).

Several instances such as this are recorded during the pre-Maccabean era. It is said that Ptolemy IV Philopator also attempted to profane the Temple but was hindered. After he had defeated Antiochus III the Great at the Battle of Raphia, the Egyptian king made a trip to Jerusalem before returning home. He entered into the Holy of Holies and was miraculously stopped in his tracks and had to be carried from the Temple.[18]

These legends suggest that prior to the time of Antiochus IV Epiphanes, the Temple was divinely protected. However, with the advent of Antiochus Epiphanes, restraint was lifted so that he did what he wished with the holy sanctuary. This is reminiscent of 2 Thessalonians 2:1-8, which suggests that all restraint will also be lifted from the Antichrist so that he will be able to do as he wishes with sacred things, appropriating them to his own nefarious ends, even to the placing of his image in the Temple with impunity.

This is just one of the many parallels between the life and times of Antiochus IV Epiphanes and the times of the Anti-

18. 3 Macc 1:9–2:24.

christ during the Great Tribulation period. We note many more of these analogies as Daniel's vision unfolds.

Daniel indicated that the days of Seleucus IV Philopator were numbered due to this sacrilege. "Within [a] few days" of Heliodorus's failure to rob the Temple "he shall be destroyed, neither in anger, nor in battle" (Dan 11:20). Seleucus Philopator was murdered, poisoned by Heliodorus.

And then there emerged one of the most unique foes which the Jews would ever face, Antiochus IV Epiphanes, with whom religious persecution and Jewish martyrdom began. The next fifteen verses in Daniel 11 are devoted to him, history's most explicit prototype of the Antichrist.

Antiochus IV Epiphanes followed his brother, Seleucus IV Philopator, on the throne of Syria in 175 B.C. His reign was destined to foreshadow the events of the Great Tribulation period.

An Analogy: The Closing Days of this Age and the Era Immediately Preceding the Reign of Antiochus IV Epiphanes

It is possible that the events of the third century B.C., which we have just reviewed in Daniel 11:5-20, may also characterize the closing days of this present age.

Everything in the first part of this vision seems to lead up to Antiochus IV Epiphanes who is the greatest precursor of the Antichrist in all Jewish literature. Preceding historical events set the stage for Antiochus's advent. However, they also may anticipate the age immediately preceding the rise of the Antichrist.

What was the outstanding feature which characterized the days before the rise of Antiochus IV Epiphanes? It is evident that those were days of conflict in which Judea was caught and squeezed like a vice between two superpowers. This theme was repeated, with some variation, throughout the entire third century B.C.

The rulers of these two superpowers follow one another in quick succession here in Daniel's prophetic documentary. Who they are matters little. Successive monarchs are called either the king of the north or the king of the south. Their individual identity is secondary, though we have identified them from the pages of ancient sources such as Appian, Diodorus Siculus, Granius Licinianus, Josephus, Justinius, Livy, Pausanias, Polybius, Strabo, the Apocrypha, and Pseudepigrapha, to name but a few. The countries over which they reigned— Syria on the north and Egypt on the south—contended with each other. Coele-Syria was the pawn between them, for the king who secured Coele-Syria, where Judea is located, controlled the land passage linking Africa, Europe, and Asia. This corridor was indispensable to trade and to military security, for this little narrow bridge between the Mediterranean Sea on the west and the Arabian Desert on the east was the only viable land link between three vast continents. Consequently, Coele-Syria was the subject of contention in this era. The nation that held Coele-Syria also held the land gate, which could be easily secured against opposing military invasion, or which could be opened and exploited for trade purposes.

A century of dispute between these superpowers, with Judea in the middle, was the context of political and military events out of which rose the most cruel and oppressive tyrant to come into focus in Daniel's vision, Antiochus IV Epiphanes. He is such a fit prototype of the Antichrist that Daniel moves easily from a preview of his reign to the reign of the Antichrist in the end days, leaving no impression that this transition is contrived.

Those third-century B.C. features are the same which are emerging in the twentieth century A.D., for Israel is still caught in a vise between two superpowers. Russia, behind the Arabs, constantly vies with the United States over the Middle East. Once again Israel is in the eye of the story, even as she was in the third century B.C.

What are the prospects for Israel today, caught in the vise of Arab antagonism which constantly threatens to draw the superpowers into hostilities over her land? Her precarious position between three great continents could lead to her demise, as it did in the days of Titus and Hadrian. Or, it could mean that we are in the End of Days, as the rabbis call it, and Israel's vise-like agony is setting the stage for the rise of the Antichrist.

In his novel, *A Beggar in Jerusalem,* Elie Wiesel records a conversation which takes place on the eve of the Six-Day War. These words reflect our day also, as well as the third century B.C., for circumstances are very similar. Its theme is the timelessness of Jewish history.

> But all agree on the outcome: we would win for lack of alternative. We had to win. The enemy could afford losing once, three times, ten times. For us, no victory would be final, while any defeat would be the last.
>
> The danger grew sharper and sharper, with the vice tightening day by day, hour by hour. The tension had long since reached the breaking point. Determined to give diplomacy its chance, the government appealed to its friends for support. The enemy saw in that a proof of weakness. What should be done? Message from Paris: above all, do not fire the first bullet. Request from Washington: above all, be patient, keep us informed. Warning from Moscow: the enemies of our friends are our enemies or will become so. The Vatican, faithful to its principles, kept silent.
>
> Meanwhile the enemy was openly preparing to attack. Former adversaries and ancient blood rivals concluded pacts and alliances, embracing before cameras, and placed their armies under joint command. The Soviet Union dispatched technicians and equipment. China promised the moral support of its masses, Algeria pledged planes and experts, Kuwait an armored division. In Arab capitals delirious mobs seethed with excitement and acclaimed the future heros of the holy war, the total war. Orators invited Jewish women

to make themselves beautiful in order to welcome the conquerors, who had clear and simple orders: burn the cities,
raze the kibbutzim, slaughter all combatants, and drown the
people of hope in an ocean of blood and fire. Words? Yes,
words. Words which evoke laughter and fear. Words which
haunt the cemeteries of Europe.[19]

19. Elie Wiesel, *A Beggar in Jerusalem*, pp. 133-34.

3

The Accession of Antiochus IV Epiphanes to the Throne

And in his place shall stand up a contemptible person, to
whom they had not given the honor of the kingdom: but
he shall come in time of security, and shall obtain the
kingdom by flatteries (Dan 11:21).

Fulfilled: 175 B.C.

DANIEL THEN SAW Antiochus IV Epiphanes rising to the
throne of Syria. This king's life, and particularly his times,
were destined to portray much that is anticipatory of the
coming Antichrist.

One of the first expositors to become aware of Daniel's
method was Saint Jerome, who wrote his Latin exposition of
the book of Daniel in the fifth century A.D. His commentary
on Daniel 11 is important in that it preserves portions of the
writings of Porphyry which otherwise would have been lost.
However, Jerome also demonstrates remarkable insight into
the nature of Daniel's prophetic method. He recognizes that
Daniel is viewing Antiochus IV Epiphanes arising in the near
future, some 300 years ahead of Daniel's day. But Jerome also
is aware that certain things Daniel saw were not fulfilled during the reign of King Antiochus Epiphanes. Many modern
critics are like Porphyry. They declare that the author of this
material is writing about events in 11:2-35 which had already
taken place, and that he was mistaken in the predictions which
he made in 11:36-45. However, Jerome preceived that the
prophet's vision of Antiochus actually merges into a view of

the Antichrist who will arise in the end days, already some 2,500 years distant from the sixth century B.C. in which Daniel lived.

Jerome says,

> Since many of the details which we are subsequently to read and explain are appropriate to the person of Antiochus, he is to be regarded as a type of the Antichrist, and those things which happened to him in a preliminary way are to be completely fulfilled in the case of the Antichrist . . . [therefore] we should also believe that the Antichrist very properly had as a type of himself the utterly wicked king, Antiochus, who persecuted the saints and defiled the Temple.[1]

THE INTRODUCTION OF ANTIOCHUS IV EPIPHANES

Viewing the accession of Antiochus IV Epiphanes to the throne of the Seleucid Empire, Daniel introduces him as "a contemptible person" (11:21).

Ancient historians were more explicit in their estimation of the new Seleucid king's character and conduct.

One such ancient source calls him "a compound of everything that was absurd and trifling . . . nothing was more vile and contemptible than the king himself."[2]

Many anecdotes from his reign reinforce this appraisal of King Antiochus.

A month-long festival of gladiatorial games was held in Daphne, a suburb of Antioch, in 166 B.C. promoted by Antiochus. Prior to this, other games were held in Macedonia, sponsored by the Roman general Aemilius Paullus. King Antiochus was "ambitious of surpassing Paullus in magnificence," says Polybius,[3] so he sent ambassadors to all the cities of Greece, inviting people to come. They flocked to Antioch in response to the king's summons. Diodorus Siculus concedes

1. Gleason L. Archer, trans., *Jerome's Commentary on Daniel*, pp. 129-30.
2. Livy *The History of Rome* 41.20.
3. Polybius *Histories* 30.5.

that Antiochus outdid all of his earlier rivals in the lavishness
of this affair. Yet his conduct during these days was scandalous,
records the ancient historian.

Antiochus organized a grand procession composed of 5,000
soldiers after the fashion of the Romans, 5,000 Mysians, a light
infantry composed of 3,000 Cilicians wearing gold crowns,
3,000 Thracians, 5,000 Gauls, and 20,000 Macedonians, half
with golden shields, one-fourth with bronze shields, and the
rest with silver shields. Following these there were 250 gladiators, then another 1,000 horsemen from Nisa, and 3,000 from
Antioch itself, wearing trappings of gold and silver. Then
came several thousand armored cavalry, preceding 100 chariots each pulled by 6 horses, 40 chariots each drawn by 4
horses, and several chariots pulled by elephants. Next were 36
more elephants, walking in single file. Eight hundred young
men wearing gold crowns escorted 1,000 fat cattle and nearly
300 cows which had been presented by various organizations
throughout the empire.

Eight hundred ivory tusks were shown in the parade. Then
came such an innumerable array of idols and images, representing every form of worship in the empire. Vast quantities
of gold and silver plate were borne by 600 slaves. The grand
parade concluded with 200 women sprinkling perfume from
golden urns upon the spectators, followed by 80 women sitting
on litters with gold feet and 500 in litters of silver. All were
richly dressed.

And then there was King Antiochus, who rode in the grand
procession, shabbily dressed, astride a sorry nag, giving orders
and attempting to direct the whole affair.[4] "But for the
diadem," says Diodorus, "no one who did not already know
him would have believed that this person was the king, lord of
the whole domain, seeing that his appearance was not even
that of an average subordinate."[5]

4. Ibid. 30.25.
5. Diodorus Siculus *Library of History* 31.16.

His conduct at the banquet was no better. He acted as a common servant, ushering people to their seats. Sometimes he would lie with the banqueters, then suddenly he would jump to his feet, tossing away his cup and plate, and, finding another group, repeat these antics. On occasion he joined the professional entertainers, jesting with them. However, the crowning insult came late in the festivities. Antiochus, wrapped in cloth, had himself carried into the banquet hall and placed on the ground by his fellow actors. Then, on cue from the orchestra, he jumped up naked and pranced about, jesting with the actors and doing an obscene dance which provoked laughter and hoots of derision.

> Diodorus says it was to the great embarrassment of the company, who all left the party in haste. Each and every person, in fact, who attended the festival found that when he regarded the extravagance of the outlay and the general management and administration of the games and processions, he was astounded, and that he admired both the king and the kingdom; when, however, he focused his attention on the king himself and his unacceptable behaviour, he could not believe that it was possible for such excellence and such baseness to exist in one and the same character.[6]

Livy, the Roman historian, says that in Antioch

> such perversity and indiscretion prevailed in his whole conduct and behaviour, that they soon changed the surname which they had given him, and instead of Epiphanes, called him Epimanes, or Madman; for many were the acts of folly or madness which he committed. . . . He allowed himself to commit the most egregious follies and the vilest indecencies in common tippling houses and in the public baths; drinking with strangers, and mingling with the lowest among the people. . . . He never thought of adhering to any rule, but rambled incessantly, adopting by turns, every kind of behaviour, insomuch, that no one could judge with certainty

6. Ibid.

as to his real character. . . . Wherefore to many he appeared
not to know what he was doing; some said that he acted from
a silly, sportive temper; others, that he was evidently mad.[7]

Athenaeus attributed his mad antics to excessive drinking,
saying that "such is the effect produced on miserable men by
want of refinement in drinking."[8]

Unknown to his guards, Antiochus would often slip out of
the palace in Antioch and walk the streets. To amuse himself
he tossed handfuls of money among the crowds and laughed
as they scrambled for it. On occasion he would act the part of
a candidate, as he had seen them do in Rome while he was a
hostage there. Embracing each of the plebeians, he would
solicit his vote as he went about the marketplace. Then, pretending election, he sat to adjudicate cases and listen to debate
on the most trivial of matters. Sometimes his friends were
completely ignored by King Antiochus, while at the same time
he would lavish expensive gifts upon total strangers. When
he did offer presents to his friends, they turned out to be a
morsel of sweetmeats, a toy, or a handful of knucklebones. If
he heard of a party anywhere in the city, he soon appeared,
without invitation, but with fife and other music. The king's
sudden appearance was so startling that some guests were
struck dumb, while others fled in terror.[9]

Polybius records the story of Antiochus's antics in the public
baths:

> He used also to bathe in the public baths, when they were
> full of townspeople, pots of the most expensive unguents
> being brought in for him; and on one occasion when some-
> one said to him, "Lucky fellows you kings, to use such things
> and smell so sweet!" without saying a word to the man, he
> waited till he was bathing the next day, and then coming in
> to the baths caused a pot of the largest size and the most

7. Livy 41.19-20.
8. Athenaeus *The Deiponoshistae* 10.439.
9. Polybius 26.10; Athenaeus 5.21; 10.52; Diodorus Siculus 29.32.

costly kind of unguent called *stacte* to be poured over his
head, so that there was a general rush of the bathers to roll
themselves in it; and when they all tumbled down, the king
himself among them, from its stickiness, there was loud
laughter.[10]

Athenaeus gives other examples of Antiochus's "crazy
doings," such as mixing wine with the city water supply in
Antioch. In addition, he would "often [have] a wreath plaited
of roses on his head," says Athenaeus, "and wearing a toga
woven of gold he would roam about all alone with stones
under his arm, which he threw at private citizens who followed
him."[11]

Antiochus's erratic behavior may have been more than eccentricity. However, some believe that the scale was tipped
from eccentricity to madness by an event which occurred during his second invasion of Egypt—called by historians the "Day
of Eleusus"—in which he had a traumatic encounter with a
representative of the Roman Senate who ordered him out of
Egypt. He was rational enough to fear the power of Rome,
but this event upset him beyond repair. From that time forward Antiochus's erratic, offensive, but harmless behavior was
turned into criminal insanity, as his malevolent attitude
toward the Jews later indicates.

Antiochus's ludicrous behavior caused ancient writers to
characterize him as a brilliant, sometimes benevolent, sometimes cruel, buffoon. In the Apocrypha he is labeled a "wicked
man" (1 Macc 1:10), while Daniel calls him "a contemptible
person," literally, one who is "despised" (Dan 11:21). The
eccentricity of Antiochus's character at the time he came to
the throne would later transform him into the most malignant
ruler that the Jews would ever encounter until the end days
when they will come into conflict with the most evil of men to
rule over them, the Antichrist, whom Antiochus prefigured.

10. Polybius 26.1.
11. Athenaeus 2.45; 10.438.

ANTIOCHUS IV EPIPHANES IN THE IMPERIAL CAPITAL: ROME

Antiochus IV Epiphanes was born in about 212 B.C., the son of Antiochus III the Great. When his father made settlement with the Romans after his disastrous defeat at the Battle of Magnesia, the conquerors required that twenty hostages be sent to Rome to guarantee the peace. The son of Antiochus III was to be included among them.

Going to Rome in his early twenties, Antiochus IV Epiphanes spent the next fourteen years as a political hostage there. Apparently he lived well while in Rome, for Asconius says that a house was provided for him at public expense.[12] Once, in after years, King Antiochus was late in paying Syria's tribute money to Rome. Finally it arrived, along with a note from the king thanking the Senate for its previous kindness toward him, saying, that "he had while in Rome, experienced so great kindness from the senate, and so much courtesy from the younger part of the community, that, among all ranks of men, he was treated as a sovereign, not as a hostage."[13]

Was Antiochus IV Epiphanes influenced in any measure by his stay in Rome?

Undoubtedly young Antiochus moved in the best circles of Roman society, and while there he was infected by a taste for western habits and ideas, and especially for western luxuries. But what about the inherent strength of Rome's political and military structure? Did it impress Antiochus in any appreciable way?

The days of Antiochus's house arrest in Rome were not in the days of the empire, of course, but the days of the Senate's supremacy. However, this was also the time in which Rome began her overseas expansion. In fact, it was the defeat of Antiochus's father, Antiochus III the Great, at Magnesia, that gave Rome her foothold in Asia. As a hostage, Antiochus Epiphanes lived in Rome on the dramatic

12. Asconius *In. Pis.* 12.
13. Livy 42.6.

eve of her emerging imperialism. There can be little doubt
that this era of expansionism greatly influenced the future
king of Syria. The Roman imperium impressed him with a
political and military structure capable of furthering the aspirations of Rome, or of Syria if Antiochus could successfully
implement them. Morkholm says,

> There can hardly be any doubt that the young Antiochus
> was impressed by what he saw and learnt in Rome, which
> had just become a recognized political center of the whole
> civilized world. A few details from his later career show that
> his stay on the banks of the Tiber was not without influence
> on his general outlook.[14]

Professor Tarn concurs, saying that Antiochus "had acquired
rather an excessive admiration for Rome's power and method."[15]

Remember the great display which Antiochus IV Epiphanes
put on in 166 b.c. in Daphne where the king raced about,
disheveled in dress and astride a sorry nag, to the embarrassment of all his constituency? Polybius says that this "festival
opened with a procession composed as follows: It was headed
by five thousand men in the prime of life, armed after the
Roman fashion and wearing breastplates of chain-armour,"[16]
indicating that in his own army Antiochus had implemented
Rome's military discipline. Some historians even contend that
Antiochus's antics in the marketplace, where he campaigned
for votes and pretended election, did not prove that he was un-
balanced, but that Antiochus was actually attempting to illus-
trate the Roman political system, and thus to teach the Roman
spirit to the citizens of Antioch.

No doubt Antiochus did have an imperialistic orientation
when he came to the throne of the Syrian Empire. Though
the Roman government was to prove a traumatic threat to him

14. Otto Markholm, *Antiochus IV of Syria,* Classical Et Mediaevalia, diss.
    8, p. 39.
15. W. W. Tarn, *The Greeks in Bactria and India,* p. 184.
16. Polybius 30.25.

in later years, he was greatly influenced by Rome's political and military prowess.

When Daniel's vision merges into the future, and the regal figure is no longer Antiochus IV Epiphanes, but the Antichrist, we learn that he, too, will arise out of an imperialistic milieu which will be oriented around the ancient Roman Empire, but in revived form. In the closing days of this age, ten nations, within the borders of the ancient Roman Empire, will form a confederation. Over these ten nations the Antichrist will gain control. Then he will build a world empire which will recapitulate the imperialistic features of the ancient Roman Empire.

However, Roman administration was not the only thing that impressed Antiochus while he was a hostage there. He was also enamored of the city itself. While the concept of the *polis* has Hellenistic overtones, the attitude of Antiochus toward his capital city of Antioch also indicates that he was interested in transplanting Roman splendor to his capital on the eastern shore of the Mediterranean.

The city of Antioch, the capital of the Seleucid Empire, was founded around 300 B.C. But when Antiochus IV Epiphanes came to the throne in 175 B.C., the city was in decline. However, the king is credited with bringing such a renaissance to the city that it was lifted to a place of cultural, economic, and political prominence never before realized. The renowned historian of Antioch, E. S. Bouchier, says,

> This extraordinary prince, with his mass of contradictory qualities, Oriental tyrant and republican Greek, low buffoon and lover of the finest art, fierce persecutor and gracious master, with his yearning for unity in government and religion which the heterogeneous Syrian kingdom was incapable of providing, may also be called the second founder of Antioch, to which he gave an impress that subsequent ages have not altogether effaced.[17]

17. E. S. Bouchier, *A Short History of Antioch, 300 B.C. to A.D. 1268*, p. 31.

He introduced gladiatorial sports of the Roman type into Antioch. The citizens, unaccustomed to this murderous sport, were disgusted by it. He had to import gladiators from Rome at great expense in order to carry on the games. Gradually the youth of Antioch became willing to undergo the rigorous training in order to participate in the games. While this cruel sport never achieved widespread acclaim in the Greek east, the more harmless chariot race and theatrical spectaculars became very popular, especially in the capital, Antioch.

Certainly it was Antiochus's admiration for Rome that moved him with determination to rival its awesome splendor in his own capital. While the city of Antioch was culturally a Greek *polis,* it was imperialist Rome in its politics and military demeanor. Antiochus was determined to cast it in that mold. Consequently, he is to be credited with the creation of a new Rome on the banks of the Orontes. While Antioch was never an actual challenge to the magnificence of Rome, nevertheless, the aim of King Antiochus was to duplicate in the east, in Antioch, what the Roman capital was in the west.

Antiochus's counterpart, the future Antichrist, will do the same when he ascends to the throne of the revived Roman Empire. His capital will be the eternal city, long in decline, but revived again in the end days to a new splendor of worldwide importance and dominion. The Antichrist will rule the world from his Roman capital situated upon the seven ancient hills. Mussolini aspired to revive the importance of this ancient capital, but where the Italian dictator failed in his demented dreams to rule the world from Rome, the Antichrist will not.

Therefore, both Antiochus IV Epiphanes and the Antichrist are to be credited with reviving the capital of an empire to imperious Roman splendor. What Antiochus did in type, the Antichrist will do in reality. However, the Antichrist's capital, revived Rome, will be as ephemeral as was ancient Rome, or Antioch, for that matter. At the coming of the Messiah the world capital will be removed from Rome to Jerusalem, where the Messiah will rule over all mankind during the last millennium of world history.

ANTIOCHUS IV EPIPHANES IN THE CULTURAL CAPITAL: ATHENS

In 176 B.C. Antiochus IV Epiphanes went to live for a while in Athens. His house arrest ended in Rome when his brother, King Seleucus IV Philopator, requested that Antiochus be released and that he be replaced by Demetrius, the oldest son of Seleucus Philopator. Perhaps this request was made for the safety of Demetrius, for it was not long after this that Seleucus Philopator was murdered. At any rate, Antiochus was then freed, and the legitimate heir to the throne of Syria was, for the time being, safe in Rome.

Antiochus was influenced politically and militarily by what he experienced while a hostage in Rome. Moving to Athens, he was then to savor a Hellenistic culture which would equally affect his administration when he finally came to the throne of the Seleucid Empire in a short time.

Appion suggests that Antiochus stayed in Athens only a few days.[18] However, most agree that, though he had been exposed to Hellenism all of his life, he remained in Athens long enough for this cultural dynamic to be confirmed in his mind as the way of life which he was to pursue.

In Rome, Greek culture had come as a mighty revelation to ' the Scipio circle among whom Antiochus spent his exile years. These Roman families reveled in everything Greek. They read Greek, spoke Greek, and lived out the Greek way of life. Antiochus, the young prince, was overpowered by Greek culture to such an extent that when he was released from Rome he went immediately to Athens, the capital of Greek culture, where he officially enrolled himself as a citizen. He may even have held some sort of public office in Athens, such as mint

18. Appian *The Syrian Wars* 65.

magistrate for the year 176-175 B.C. In that year, Athenian coins bore his symbol, the elephant.[19] At any rate, he was well known to the Athenians, for they later erected statues of him in the agora, apparently in gratitude to King Antiochus for certain benefits he had promised them while living there.[20] A broken inscription found in Pergamum is believed to be a copy of an Athenian decree thanking Emuenes II for his aid in placing Antiochus on the throne of Syria.[21]

Margolis and Marx remark that "the Seleucid rulers in general were admirers of Greek culture; but this Antiochus... was an enthusiast, proud of his Athenian citizenship, and bent upon spreading Hellenic civilization in his domains."[22] It was his Athenian experience which must have sold. Antiochus on the dissemination of the Greek way of life among the countries of the east, wherever his empire might extend.

Ten years later and a thousand miles away in Judea, this sophisticated depravity which Antiochus had imbibed in Rome, and the dynamism of which had been confirmed in Athens, would be forced upon Jerusalem. The result would be horrible for the Jews. However, it was this same Hellenistic current which would finally destroy the unity of his empire. The unity which Antiochus in these early days thought to lie in the solidifying effects of Hellenism would ultimately rob him of his rule over the Jews, for it was against this very Hellenism that the Maccabees revolted.

While Alexander the Great introduced Hellenistic culture into the east, and while the universal use of the Greek language disseminated it among all the nations of the east, it was not until the reign of King Antiochus Epiphanes that Hellenism was forced upon a people. The resulting pressure of an

19. William B. Dinsmoor, "The Repair of the Athena Parthenos," in *American Journal of Archaeology* (1934), p. 105.
20. Markholm, p. 40.
21. Edwyn R. Bevan, "Syria and the Jews," in *The Cambridge Ancient History*, 8:487.
22. Max Margolis, and Alexander Marx, *A History of the Jewish People*, p. 135.

enforced Greek lifestyle upon the Jews was to blow the empire apart in Coele-Syria.

But during those early days in Athens, Antiochus had no way of knowing the devastating results which Hellenism would have upon the solidarity of his empire in later years. He only saw the beauty and political stability it had brought to one city, Athens. Surely it could do the same with many cities and ultimately produce this same beauty and political stability throughout his empire.

ANTIOCHUS IV EPIPHANES IN HIS ROYAL CAPITAL: ANTIOCH

It was while Antiochus IV Epiphanes was living in Athens that his brother, Seleucus IV Philopator, was murdered. There were three possible claimants to the throne of Syria: Seleucus's son, Demetrius, then a hostage in Rome; an infant son, also named Antiochus; and Antiochus Epiphanes himself.

But, with no one immediately present to claim the throne, Heliodorus—who probably instigated the murder of the king in the first place—assumed the crown and attempted to reign as king regent in the place of the infant Antiochus.

But when the news of Seleucus's death reached Athens, Antiochus IV Epiphanes, the child's uncle and the only adult in the house of Seleucus, made ready to seize the throne. Having no army to back his claim, Antiochus appealed to the king of Pergamum for aid. Persuaded to help him, Emuenes II, king of Pergamum, escorted Antiochus with an army to Syria, ejected Heliodorus, and established the new king on the throne of the Seleucid Empire.

It was Antiochus's unnatural accession to the throne which Daniel saw in his vision. In the place of Seleucus IV Philopator, he said, "shall stand up a contemptible person, to whom they had not given the honor of the kingdom: but he shall come in time of security, and shall obtain the kingdom by flatteries" (11:21).

It was by flattery—some plausible representation the nature of which we do not know—that Antiochus IV Epiphanes obtained the throne. His flatteries were probably directed to Emuenes II, king of Pergamum. Antiochus could easily exploit Emuenes' need for a friend on the throne of Syria in case of a showdown with the Romans. Appian hints at this, saying that Heliodorous "was driven out by Emuenes and Attalus, who installed Antiochus therein in order to secure his goodwill; for, by reason of certain bickerings, they also had already grown suspicious of the Romans."[23] Therefore, by flattery, Antiochus persuaded King Emuenes to aid him in taking over the government of Syria.

Upon ascending to the throne of the Seleucid Empire, Antiochus was immediately confronted with a series of crises. His financial situation was always desperate. The Seleucid monarchy was never as financially sound as was the Ptolemaic. At the close of the reign of Antiochus III the Great, the treasury had been depleted by his disastrous war with Rome, When Seleucus IV Philopator came to the throne, not only was the treasury empty, but also Syria was saddled with an impossible war indemnity to Rome which had to be paid annually from an empty treasury. Antiochus IV Epiphanes attempted to supplement regular income by systematically robbing the temples throughont his empire. His father, Antiochus III the Great, had been killed trying this method of raising revenue; however, King Antiochus Epiphanes successfully relieved many temples of their wealth, including the Temple in Jerusalem.

A second and rather constant crisis was the lack of cohesion in his empire. Antiochus's subject nations were a heterogeneous lot. This disunity was met by the king's rigorous policy of hellenization which worked everywhere, except among the Jews of Judea.

In addition, at the beginning of his reign there were three nations which posed a threat to him. Before any stability

23. Appian, 45.

could be realized, Antiochus had to deal with them. Professor Russell says, "The empire which he inherited lacked cohesion and was in danger of breaking up, his neighbours the Egyptians, the Romans, and the Parthians were pressing in upon him from every side, ready to take the utmost advantage of Syria's weakness."[24] The problem of these three enemy nations had to be attended to before King Antiochus could hope to stabilize the crown. To attempt a solution, he invaded Egypt several times at the beginning of his reign. He placated Rome throughout his reign. And, finally he died, still trying to solve the Parthian problem at the end of his reign.

There is a subtle parallel here between the beginning of Antiochus's reign and the institution of the Antichrist upon the throne of the revived Roman Empire, for the Antichrist also will face a threefold international threat when he comes to reign. Though we do not know which three nations are to be involved, we do know that there will be the same number of nations to resist the Antichrist as those who opposed Antiochus Epiphanes. These three nations must be subdued before the universal reign of the Antichrist can be confirmed. Daniel views this three-nation opposition to the Antichrist, the little horn, in apocalyptic terms.

> After this I saw in the night-visions, and, behold, a fourth beast, terrible and powerful, and strong exceedingly; and it had great iron teeth; it devoured and brake in pieces, and stamped the residue with its feet: and it was diverse from all the beasts that were before it; and it had ten horns. I considered the horns, and, behold, there came up among them another horn, a little one, before which three of the first horns were plucked up by the roots: and, behold, in this horn were eyes like the eyes of a man, and a mouth speaking great things. . . . Thus he said, The fourth beast shall be a fourth kingdom . . . and shall devour the whole earth, and

24. D. S. Russell, *The Jews from Alexander to Herod*, in The Clarendon Bible, 5:31.

shall tread it down, and break it in pieces. And as for the ten horns, out of this kingdom shall ten kings arise: and another shall arise after them; and he shall be diverse from the former, and he shall put down three kings (Dan 7:7-8, 23-24).

During the first year of Belshazzar, while the Babylonian Empire still maintained universal dominion in the east, Daniel saw four beasts rising out of the sea. Each of these beasts represented one of the four great Gentile world powers which would succeed each other in the course of history.

First, a lionlike beast appeared, an apocalyptic representation of the Babylonian Empire. This was followed by a bear, representing the Persian Empire. This second empire replaced Babylon in world dominion even while Daniel was still living to see this phase of his vision fulfilled. Third, the leopard with four wings and four heads emerged. This, as we have previously noted, was Alexander the Great and His Greek empire. Then a fourth beast, terrible and powerful, appeared. This was the final Gentile world power to arise in the ancient world, Rome. As the prophet watched, ten horns emerged, followed by an eleventh, a little horn, which pushed its way up in the midst of the ten. The little horn plucked up three of these surrounding ten horns by the roots. As Daniel watched the activity of the little horn subduing its opposition, suddenly,

I beheld till thrones were placed, and one that was ancient of days did sit: his raiment was white as snow, and the hair of his head like pure wool: his throne was fiery flames, and the wheels thereof burning fire. A fiery stream issued and came forth from before him: thousands of thousands ministered unto him, and ten thousand times ten thousand stood before him: the judgment was set, and the books were opened. I beheld at that time because of the voice of the great words which the horn spake; I beheld even till the beast was slain, and its body destroyed, and it was given to be burned with fire (Dan 7:9-11).

The fourth beast, which represented the Roman Empire, was the real subject of the vision, for Daniel asked specifically for an explanation of this beast, its ten horns, the emerging little horn, and its conflict with the three horns which were plucked up (7:19).

It seems clear that the ancient Roman Empire must revive again in the last days since the advent of the Messiah is presented in the context of an extant Roman Empire. The prophet Daniel, consistent with all Old Testament prophecy, did not see the age of the Church which intervenes between the first and second coming of Christ. Therefore, the decline and fall of the ancient Roman Empire were unseen by Daniel. He saw only the fourth beast, the Roman Empire, which existed in the ancient world, and its revived form, which will be in existence when the Messiah comes in glorious reign, but not the age of the Church which separates the two.

The spirit of Rome demonstrated its capacity to rejuvenate in the Renaissance. That same viable spirit will bring forth the Roman Empire again in the end days. The ten horns represent a ten-nation confederation which will constitute the revived Roman Empire. Out of these the Antichrist, the little horn, will arise. But he must subdue three of these nations, the three horns plucked up, before his universal reign can be stabilized. Having plucked them up by the roots, he will then reign until the advent of the Messiah puts an end to his empire.

Thus, what Antiochus IV Epiphanes confronted at the beginning of his reign—the three-nation opposition—the Antichrist also will confront at the beginning of his reign. King Antiochus never really succeeded in eliminating his antagonists, the three-nation opposition of Egypt, Rome, and Parthia. The Antichrist will, however, make quick dispatch of his three horn antagonists. These nations will be rapidly subdued, and the Antichrist will rule over the ten horns, the ten-nation confederation which will make up the revived Roman Empire of the last days.

In conclusion, in 175 B.C. a king came to the throne of the Seleucid Empire whose life and times parallel the reign of the future Antichrist with such accuracy that it is without precedent. Consequently, it was natural for Daniel to move in his vision from the one to the other. This is why we view the reign of King Antiochus IV Epiphanes as a foreshadowing of the reign of the Antichrist during the end days, the era of great persecution which will immediately precede the coming of Israel's Messiah.

4

Judea During the First Years of Antiochus's Reign

And the overwhelming forces shall be overwhelmed from before him, and shall be broken; yea, also the prince of the covenant. And after the league made with him he shall work deceitfully; for he shall come up, and shall become strong, with a small people. In time of security shall he come even upon the fattest places of the province; and he shall do that which his fathers have not done, nor his fathers' fathers; he shall scatter among them prey, and spoil, and substance: yea, he shall devise his devices against the strongholds, even for a time (Dan 11:22-24).

Fulfilled: 175-170 B.C.

THE VERSES now under consideration cover that period of time *after* Antiochus IV Epiphanes came to the throne (11:21) and *before* his first invasion of Egypt (11:25). The dates for the fulfillment of this part of Daniel's vision are 175-170 B.C., and his frame of reference is "the province," the circumstances in Judea during this interim.

These verses are descriptive of Antiochus's general approach to securing his throne in all the provinces of his empire where he found it necessary to exercise additional precaution, or where the area was particularly explosive. However, they are uniquely apropos to Judea and to the tactics which King Antiochus used there. Daniel's mention of the prince of the covenant, that is, the Jewish high priest, also indicates that Judea comes into view here.

These years were preliminary to the great persecution which Antiochus IV Epiphanes imposed upon the Jews following 170 B.C. They were marked by a "time of security" (11:24; cf. v. 21) and involved the threefold stratagem which Antiochus apparently used throughout his empire for securing his throne.

First, there was the elimination of the orthodox religious leadership (11:22*b*) followed by the infiltration of a small group of deceivers and subverters (11:23). Finally, he purchased the allegiance of his important subjects with bribery (11:24).

These intrigues were applied to Judea. However, they failed to produce the internal results that the king expected. When, after five years, the Jews were not yet fully submissive to him, Antiochus turned to direct persecution (11:30-35).

This same maneuver will be implemented by the Antichrist, who also will turn upon the Jews during a time of security during the end days. The Antichrist will replace the Jewish high priest with a false prophet, just as Antiochus replaced the legitimate high priest, Onias III, with Jason and finally with Menelaus. In Antiochus's day many of the Jews became Hellenistic subverters. During the reign of the Antichrist there will also be Jews who will join the cult of the beast and subvert their fellow Jews. In addition, the Antichrist will divide the land and distribute it among his followers in order to secure their allegiance, just as King Antiochus apparently did.

ANTIOCHUS DISRUPTS THE TIME OF SECURITY

And the overwhelming forces shall be overwhelmed from before him, and shall be broken (Dan 11:22*a*).

Daniel's imagery is one of deluge, for he saw armies surging back and forth across the land like a sweeping flood. These forces are called "armies of the flood" in the Hebrew text. All resistance collapsed before Antiochus. The opposition in view here was probably the domestic forces of Heliodorus which made a final effort to retain the king regent upon the throne, but to no avail.

Antiochus IV Epiphanes became king of the Seleucid Empire in 175 B.C. Twice Daniel notes that the hostilities which erupted in association with Antiochus's accession to the throne came in a "time of security" (11:21, 24). The relative peace which King Antiochus interrupted had lasted for nearly a quarter of a century. Prior to that, for almost the entire third century B.C., the Ptolemies and Seleucids had fought with each other, much of the time across the land of the Jews.

However, the conflict ended in 198 B.C. when Antiochus III the Great appeared before the gates of Jerusalem and was given a warm reception by the city elders. The Judeans promised supplies for the victorious Syrian army and even helped them dispel the remaining Egyptian garrison in Jerusalem. As a result, Antiochus the Great guaranteed the unique position of the Jews in a letter he wrote to the governor of the province. This letter was preserved by Josephus.[1] It laid the foundation for the peaceful existence of the Jews within the Seleucid kingdom, and for the next twenty-five years the Jews were left to pursue their destiny in relative freedom. It was this epistle of Antiochus the Great which guaranteed the "time of security" to which Daniel refers in verses 21 and 24. During this era the Seleucid king, Antiochus III the Great, and his son, Seleucus IV Philopator, even participated in Jewish sacrifices by making contributions to the Temple (2 Macc 3:3).

In addition, Antiochus the Great provided for the repair of the Temple, plus the remission of taxes for three years, and commanded the return of Jewish slaves. He also forbade any Gentile to desecrate the Temple, saying, "It shall be lawful for no foreigner to come within the limits of the temple round about; which thing is forbidden also to the Jews, unless to those who, according to their own custom, have purified them-

1. Josephus *Antiquities* 12.3.3.

selves."² Furthermore, Antiochus the Great restricted any animal that was not kosher from being brought into the city of Jerusalem.

In another letter, King Antiochus III the Great revealed that his reasons for these concessions to the Jews was in order "that by enjoying the effects of our humanity, they may show themselves the more willing and ready about our affairs. Take care likewise of that nation, as far as thou are able, that they may not have any disturbance given them by any one."³

And then, Antiochus IV Epiphanes destroyed the "time of security" which his father had insured the Jews nearly a quarter of a century earlier.

The time of security which the future Antichrist will break is also protected by a covenant. When the Antichrist comes to reign over the ten-nation confederation which will compose the revived Roman Empire of the last days, he will make a covenant with Israel. Under the terms of Antiochus's covenant with the Jews, the Temple was to be repaired. But under the Antichrist's covenant, the Temple will be rebuilt and the Levitical priesthood and sacrifices reinstituted. Many of the concessions which Antiochus III the Great made in his day will reappear in the covenant to be made between the Antichrist and Israel. However, this covenant will be broken (Dan 9:27) and the time of security which it will have inaugurated will be shattered (8:25), just as it was in the time of King Antiochus Epiphanes.

THE ELIMINATION OF A GREAT RELIGIOUS LEADER

And shall be broken; yea, also the prince of the covenant (Dan 11:22b).

We now relate the tactics which Antiochus IV Epiphanes may have used throughout his empire to the circumstances in Judea to see how they were enforced there.

2. Ibid.
3. Ibid., 12.3.4.

The first of these tactics had to do with the religious leadership. The machinations of Antiochus led him to destroy the prince of the covenant.

It can be argued that Antiochus did not himself destroy the prince, for, in actuality, it was the Hellenistic Jews who did so. The sequence of events grew out of the opposition of the Tobiads to the high priest, Onias III. Things became so serious in Jerusalem between the hellenizing Tobiad family and Onias that the high priest had to go to Antioch to plead his case before King Seleucus IV Philopator. Onias was under suspicion of treason. He had to explain to the king that his opposition to Heliodorus was not treasonable, as the Tobiads would make it seem, for he was acting in accord with the promise of Antiochus III the Great who had guaranteed the sanctity of the Temple over a quarter of a century earlier.[4]

However, Seleucus IV Philopator died while Onias was still in Antioch. The new king, Antiochus Epiphanes, then removed Onias from office, not because of a conscious effort at this point in history to subvert the Jews' religion, but because he was offered money for the high priesthood by another Jew. Furthermore, Onias was subsequently murdered, but not by King Antiochus. A fellow Jew did it. While this is the case historically, Daniel still charges Antiochus with breaking the prince of the covenant, for, ultimately, the king himself was responsible for Onias's fall. He presumed to vacate the high priesthood and to fill it contrary to Jewish tradition.

This is the first phase of the program for subduing the Jews. While his military ascendancy over the Jews was merely a perpetuation of the Seleucid dominion which had existed since 198 B.C., the king's aspirations went deeper. There grew in Antiochus, as time passed, a desire to possess the soul of the Jew. To implement this plot, King Antiochus initiated his first device, which was to rid the Jews of the legitimate religious leader who personified their will to spiritual resistance.

4. Solomon Zeitlin, *The Rise and Fall of the Judean State*, 1:76.

Although internal turmoil in Judah, centering around the conflict between the house of Onias and the house of Tobias, aided in the overthrow of the rigidly orthodox high priest by the Hellenistic Tobiads, Antiochus was ultimately responsible for deposing this religious leadership, Onias, the prince of the covenant, whom Daniel saw broken.

It came about like this: Onias III had resisted the attempts of Heliodorus to rob the Temple of its treasures. It was also his cousin Simon who had revealed the presence of the Temple treasure. Now antagonism between Onias and Simon intensified until Onias was afraid that civil strife would break out in Jerusalem. In addition, Simon also had caused the governor of Syria, Apollonius, to suspect the high priest of treason. It was at this point, about 176-175 b.c., that Onias set out for Antioch.

The conflict went deeper than a power struggle between Onias III and Simon, however, for they represented two strong houses, the Oniads and the Tobiads. These two houses, in turn, stood for opposing views about Judaism itself. Onias and his associates sought to perpetuate a traditional Judaism according to the precepts of the Torah and the prophets. They were opposed to foreign cultural influences. The Tobiads had given up all interest in traditional Judaism. They were Greek in outlook and interested in replacing the rigid Judaism of their fathers with a relaxed Hellenism.

The members of the Tobias family also were leaders of a new aristocracy of wealth in Jerusalem. Their economic interests could prosper only if Jerusalem became a Hellenistic city. They also knew that as long as Onias III was high priest he would resist Hellenism. Consequently, the Tobiads conspired to have Onias replaced by his brother, Joshua, who was more disposed to the Greek way of life and even bore a Greek name, Jason.

It was about this time, when Onias III set out for Antioch, that Seleucus IV Philopator was murdered by Heliodorus, and

Antiochus IV Epiphanes, the new king, came to the throne. The Apocrypha tells what happened next:

> But when Seleucus was dead and had been succeeded by Antiochus, known as Epiphanes, Jason, Onias's brother, obtained the high-priesthood by corrupt means. He petitioned the king and promised him three hundred and sixty talents in silver coin immediately, and eighty talents from future revenue. In addition he undertook to pay another hundred and fifty talents for the authority to institute a sports-stadium, to arrange for the education of young men there, and to enrol in Jerusalem a group to be known as the 'Antiochenes.' The king agreed, and, as soon as he had seized the high-priesthood, Jason made the Jews conform to the Greek way of life (2 Macc 4:7-10).

Antiochus, the new king, had only recently come to Syria from Rome and Athens. Very quickly he built up an aversion to Judaism which would later explode in his terrorizing pogroms against the Jews. Now he was gratified that Jason, a Jew, was interested in spreading Greek culture among his fellow Jews. Therefore, King Antiochus made his first move toward the hellenization of Judaism. He sold the office of the high priest to Jason.

Josephus says that Onias III fled to Egypt in order to escape Antiochus IV Epiphanes.[5] But 2 Maccabees (4:33) states that he sought refuge in a heathen temple in Daphne in the suburbs of Antioch. This was about 175 B.C. A few years later, in about 171 B.C., Onias was lured from his sanctuary and killed.

While not directly responsible for the death of Onias III, King Antiochus is nevertheless credited with deposing Onias, the prince of the covenant, when he sold the office to Jason. By this act the Syrian king virtually abolished the spiritual significance of the ancient office of high priest, thereby relieving it of any orthodox opposition to his Hellenistic intentions for

5. Josephus *Wars* 7.10.2.

Judea. "Henceforth," says Professor Tcherikover, "the candidate paid the king the price of the position, so that in consequence the High Priesthood had become a normal official post and the High Priest a Seleucid royal official utterly dependent upon the king for favor."[6]

Jason not only bought the office of high priest, but implicit in his offer was his determination to hellenize the Jews. When Antiochus accepted Jason's offer and granted him the high priesthood, the king also gave him leave to hellenize the Jews by transforming the city of Jerusalem into a Greek *polis*. Jerusalem was even renamed Antioch.[7] By this act Antiochus broke the covenant and abolished the privileges granted to the Jews under his father, Antiochus III the Great, which assured them of their right to live according to their customs. In place of Jewish tradition, Greek law was introduced.

> They built a sports-stadium in the gentile style in Jerusalem.
> They removed their marks of circumcision and repudiated
> the holy covenant. They intermarried with Gentiles, and
> abandoned themselves to evil ways. . . . So Hellenism reached
> a high point with the introduction of foreign customs
> through the boundless wickedness of the impious Jason, no
> true high priest. As a result, the priests no longer had any
> enthusiasm for their duties at the altar, but despised the
> temple and neglected the sacrifices; and in defiance of the
> law they eagerly contributed to the expenses of the wrestling-
> school whenever the opening gong called them. They placed
> no value on their hereditary dignities, but cared about
> everything for Hellenic honours (1 Macc 1:14-15; 2 Macc
> 4:13-15).

During this era, Anitochus IV Epiphanes visited Jerusalem and was received with great honor (2 Macc 4:22).

Any process of hellenization had to focus upon the cities, for the dissemination of Greek culture was urban in strategy.

6. Victor Tcherikover, *Hellenistic Civilization of the Jews*, pp. 160-61.
7. Abraham Schalit, ed., *The Hellenistic Age*, 6:125.

Hellenism would have died in the east had not Alexander the Great built cities to accommodate it. This is the environment which it needed in order to flourish. If cities were not readily available, then they had to be built. This made Alexander and his successors city builders on a grand scale. Alexander also brought masses of Macedonian soldiers to settle in these new eastern cities, as well as in older, established ones. These Macedonian veterans were located in crucial cities all the way to India.

In Syria, Alexander and his successors followed this plan of urbanization. However, not many new cities like Alexandria were necessary. Rather, the already existing cities were redeveloped into Hellenistic types. Names of cities, in addition to Jerusalem, were changed. The Old Testament Aleppo became Acre, for example.

Jason's hellenization program for Jerusalem was not progressing fast enough, however, to suit the Tobiads who wanted the city thoroughly hellenized and internationalized as quickly as possible in order to facilitate economics. The larger cities of the coast already had gone Greek. Cities in Phoenicia, for example, had become Greek cities during the preceding century. So had the Philistine cities. All Hellenistic cities were linked by a common orientation which brought them into productive contact with the central government of the Seleucid Empire. The economy was stimulated by this, and the wealthy upper class was further enriched. Therefore, the Tobiads were concerned that Jerusalem participate in the international life of the Hellenistic world. To speed up this process, they picked Menelaus, Simon's brother, to become the high priest. Their opportunity came when Jason sent Menelaus up to Antioch to pay the tribute money owed to King Antiochus.

Though Menelaus was a Benjamite who had no claim on the office whatsoever (2 Macc 3:4; 3:24), nevertheless he procured the office by using the same ruse which Jason had used

three years before. He offered Antiochus 300 talents of silver
more than Jason was currently paying.

Menelaus returned to Jerusalem as the new high priest and,
with the aid of Syrian soldiers, ejected Jason from the city.
Under him the policy of hellinization proceeded unabetted.
In fact, it was Menelaus who suggested that the king force
Hellenism upon the Jews. Graetz says that Menelaus advised
Antiochus IV Epiphanes

> to destroy Judaism root and branch, and to force its ad-
> herents to adopt the Greek cults. Antiochus, who hated both
> the Judaeans and their religion, was well pleased with the
> suggestion of Menelaus, and determined to carry it into
> execution with his characteristic tenacity. He must over-
> come not only the Judean people, but also the Judean God.[8]

Menelaus also instigated the death of Onias III.

It was possible that Onias is the teacher of righteousness
who appears in the Dead Sea Scrolls, while Menelaus is the
wicked prince who opposes him. When Menelaus fell behind
in his payments for the high priest's office, he received a royal
summons to Antioch. Before he could get there, however,
King Antiochus left for Cilicia, placing Andronicus in charge
of things until he could return. To pay his debt, Menelaus
stole some gold plate from the Temple in Jerusalem. For this
sacrilege, Onias, who was still living in exile in Antioch, denounced him publicly. It was then that Menelaus conspired
with Andronicus to have Onias murdered. When King Antiochus returned to his capital, he learned of Onias's death and
"shed tears of pity."[9] He also had Andronicus put to death
for his part in the murder. But Menelaus remained free and,
returning to Jerusalem, continued his hellenization of the
Jews.

Though Antiochus may not have seen the advantages of

---

8. H. Graetz, *A Popular History of the Jews,* 1:345-46.
9. Edwyn R. Bevan, "Syria and the Jews," *The Cambridge Ancient History,*
   8:504.

owning the high priest at first—the sale of the office for additional revenue was his initial interest in the high priesthood—he later realized the advantages of possessing the religious leadership in Jerusalem in order to promote more effectively his policy of hellenization.

In the last days the Antichrist will also have the assistance of a great religious leader to aid him in the promotion of his plans for world dominion. Furthermore, the false prophet will abet the Antichrist in realizing his aspirations to be worshiped as God. Where King Antiochus had two successive religious leaders who were dedicated to subverting the Jews to Hellenism, the Antichrist will have but one. However, the false prophet will comprehend in himself all the subversive talents of both Jason and Menelaus and will utilize them during the Great Tribulation period to coerce many Jews into submitting to the cult of the beast. The false prophet is presented in Revelation 13:11-18. He is the beast whom John saw arising out of the earth. The Antichrist will rise out of the sea (Rev 13:1) and probably will be a Gentile. But the false prophet will rise out of the land (13:11) and probably will be an apostate Jew.

Jesus indicated that the false religious leaders always arise in times of crisis, just as they did during the Antiochus crisis of 175 to 164 b.c., during the Roman crisis of the first century, and during the expulsion crisis of the Middle Ages when Jews were being evicted from countries like Spain and England. They also will arise during the last days (Matt 24:24). However, the false prophet will head all the apostate religious subversion which will emerge during the final crisis, the reign of the Antichrist.

There is no scriptural proof that the office of high priest will be revived in the end days. However, since there is an abundance of biblical evidence that the Temple will be rebuilt and the Levitical system of sacrifices and offerings reinstituted, it seems mandatory that the priesthood will be revived and a high priest appointed. Perhaps this is the reason that those Jews who are Cohanim have kept their Levitical lineage in tact through the centuries, while all other Jews have lost their tribal identity.

During the Great Tribulation when the Antichrist will break his covenant with the Jews and terminate the Temple worship, the office of the high priest will again be subverted by this Gentile ruler. He will replace the legitimate high priest with an impostor, the false prophet.

The false prophet, who will be to the Antichrist what Menelaus was to Antiochus IV Epiphanes, will be dedicated to coercing everyone to worship the beast. His fellow Jews will have to either yield to the cult of the beast, receive his mark, and worship him, or be killed, just as Menelaus coerced the Jews of his day into the virtual worship of Antiochus through submission to Hellenism. Some resisted. They were called Hasidim, "the pious ones." They were hounded and killed until the time that the great deliverer, Judas Maccabee, appeared. Others, like the Hellenistic Jews, yielded to Menelaus and to the hellenizing edicts of King Antiochus. They survived but at the price of their souls.

THE TECHNIQUE OF DECEIT

> And after the league made with him he shall work deceit-
> fully; for he shall come up, and shall become strong, with
> a small people (Dan 11:23).

Daniel's next observation about the tactics which Antiochus IV Epiphanes utilized in order to secure his throne is his use of deceit. This deception was implemented through a small group.

Though this technique must have been used by King Antiochus in various parts of his empire, Professor Montgomery recognizes that it had a special application to the Jews. He says, "Explicit historical reference need not be sought, beyond the Jews' experience of the king's art in playing off the local

parties against one another, e.g., Jason against Onias, Menelaus against Jason."[10]

Here is the use of a small group to deceive the many into
submission. This is the strategy which Karl Marx worked out
as he sat in the British Museum writing his directives for com-
munist take-over. It is the scenario which has been played out
in every country that has capitulated to Communism.

One of the first times that this stratagem was used was in the
second century b.c. when Orthodox Judaism was infiltrated
by Hellenists. The last time that this trick will be applied
is during the end days when the orthodox religious community of the Jews will be subverted to the cult of the beast by a
small group of contemporary Jewish apostates.

The Hellenistic subverters in Antiochus's day were drawn
from among the wealthy. These Jews promoted Hellenism for
economic advantages. Many of the priests were wealthy aristo-
crats and many of these aristocratic priests became Hellenists.
They were the "small people," that is, "the few men,"[11] whom
King Antiochus used to undermine religious tradition and orthodoxy in Judea. Professor Hengel says of this minority:

> For by and large the events between 175 and 167 b.c. which
> began with the introduction of gymnasium education and
> ended with the 'abomination of desolation' marked a unique
> and deep turning point in the history of Palestinian Judaism,
> during the Graeco-Roman period. Only in that brief space
> of about eleven years under the rule of Antiochus IV was
> Judaism in the acute danger of submitting to Hellenistic
> culture as the result of the assimilation furthered by a power-
> ful aristocratic minority.[12]

Specifically, Hellenism posed a threefold threat to Orthodox
Judaism. First, in order to qualify for the status of a Hellenis-

10. James A. Montgomery, *A Critical and Exegetical Commentary on the
    Book of Daniel,* in The International Critical Commentary, p. 451.
11. A. Bevan, *A Short Commentary on the Book of Daniel for the Use of
    Students,* p. 187.
12. Martin Hengel, *Judaism and Hellenism,* 1:77.

tic city, Jerusalem had to erect and maintain the typical institutions which made up the Hellenistic metropolis: the
agora, stadium, hippodrome, but particularly the gymnasium.
A gymnasium was more than a place for exercise in the
Greek *polis,* for in it verbal, as well as physical, contest took
place. It was a place of debate and learning. It was an institution in which the young were educated in the appreciation
of all the Hellenistic values. While the emphasis was upon
the development of physical form, much else transpired in the
gymnasium to influence Jewish youth in the Greek way of life.
This chief mark of the Greek *polis* soon appeared on Mount
Moriah (2 Macc 4:12), where the gymnasium and the Temple
lay in close proximity.

Jewish youths horrified their elders by exercising in the
nude according to Greek custom. Homosexuality—accepted
by the Greeks as one of the highest forms of human love—may
have made inroads among the youth who frequented the gymnasium. The priests also were enticed by the Greek games and
neglected their duty in order to frequent the gymnasium. This
was a scandal because, at this period in Judaism, nudity was
considered a sin. The contemporary book of Jubilees says,
"All those who know the judgment of the law that they should
cover their shame and should not uncover themselves as the
Gentiles uncover themselves" (3:31).

Possibly Greek teachers were employed to train Judean
youths for participation in the Olympic games. Since Greek
custom demanded that the participant in the athletic games
appear nude in the public, "Judean youth had to learn to
suppress their sense of shame," says Graetz, "and to expose
their bodies in the sight of the very Temple in which no steps
to the altar were permitted that the nakedness of the body
might not be visible."[13]

But soon, in this environment of the gymnasium, these

13. Graetz, 1:336.

Jewish youths who were won to the Greek way became ashamed of everything Jewish. They dressed like Greeks. They donned the broad brim hat; the chlamys, a short woolen mantel worn by men; and the high-laced boots. Such attire was seen everywhere in Jerusalem. These Jews spoke Greek and read Greek books, and, because their circumcision was a public embarrassment to them, some even sought to have its effects surgically reversed. "Others," says Josephus, "hid the circumcision of their genitals, that even when they were naked they might appear to be Greeks. Accordingly, they left off all the customs that belonged to their own country, and imitated the practice of other nations."[14]

While the gymnasium presented the first Hellenistic threat to traditional Judaism, a second threat emerged. It was the open society of the Greeks. Now assimilation could be a real danger. Baalam said of Israel,

> Lo, it is a people that dwelleth alone, and shall not be reckoned among the nations (Num 23:9).

Philo, expounding this passage, said, "Israel shall be apart not so much by reason of the separation of their home or the cutting off of their land, but by reason of the peculiarity of their customs, for they shall not mix with other peoples, so that they may not deviate from their distinctive way of life."[15] However, the Greek concept of the universal man could not long tolerate Jewish provincialism. If the Jews were Hellenized they would also be universalized, absorbed into the Greek world, and the peculiar covenant people of God would be no more.

Due to the Hellenistic threat to Judaism's uniqueness, the Hasidim, forerunners of the Pharisees, emerged at this time. The New Testament Pharisees as well as the Hasidim, their second-century B.C. predecessors, were separatists who main-

14. Josephus *Antiquities* 12.5.1.
15. Philo *De Vita Mosis* 2.24.

tained a vigil against the assimilation which Hellenism threatened.

The third threat was philosophical. Hellenism enticed the Jews to exchange their "Thus saith the LORD" for a vapid sophistry. The unchanging moral Law of Mount Sinai would be replaced by the rationalism of the Athenian Acropolis. At issue was the authority for ethical conduct. Does its authority lie in reason, as the Greeks affirmed, or is it the authority of revelation, as the Jews declared? Is man the measure and therefore all ethical conduct relative, as the Greeks would have it; or is the course of ethical conduct absolute and unbending, as Judaism maintained? Is truth propositional as found in the Torah, or is it derived through reason and contained in the dialectics of Plato, Aristotle, and other Greek philosophers?

The faithful Jews were encouraged to yield Jerusalem's theocracy to Athens' secular democracy. They were enticed to give up their monotheism and adopt a foreign polytheism. Revelation was to give way to reason, and they were to exchange the intangible holiness of Judaism for the tangible beauty of Hellenism. Since a synthesis of Hellenism and Judaism was impossible; a clash was inevitable.

In the end days, under the universal reign of the Antichrist, Orthodox Judaism will once again clash with a subtle threat similar to Hellenism. And just as this new religion in the second century B.C. was propagated by the hellenizing party among the Jews, a relatively small group, so the subversive religion of the last days will be similarly propagated. Jesus singled out these false religious subversives in His great prophetic discourse and warned against them (Matt 24:4-5, 11, 24).

LOYALTY SECURED BY BRIBERY

In time of security shall he come even upon the fattest places of the province; and he shall do that which his fathers have not done, nor his fathers' fathers; he shall scatter among them prey, and spoil, and substance: yea, he shall devise his devices against the strongholds, even for a time (Dan 11:24).

Daniel indicates that Antiochus IV Epiphanes would do something unique which previous monarchs had not done. He would lavish gifts upon individuals and communities in order to secure their loyalty. Diodorus Siculus confirms this, saying, "Antiochus, on first succeeding to the throne, embarked upon a quixotic mode of life foreign to other monarchs."[16] Diodorus then details the extravagances in which Antiochus engaged during the forays among the citizens of Antioch. Driver says that by these antics Antiochus was "courting popularity to an excessive degree."[17]

His generosity to people in foreign provinces was no less noteworthy. Polybius says that in one of his Egyptian campaigns he ordered that a gold piece be given to every Greek in the captured city of Naukratis.[18] This may have been his policy in every Egyptian city which he had captured during his first campaign. Bevan believes that this was the reason why Antiochus had special coins minted: to commemorate his conquest and his generosity. All of these coins which have survived are in bronze. But his gift of gold coin to the Greek citizens of Naukratis may indicate that he especially favored that city.[19]

In addition, King Antiochus's municipal generosity was most amazing. He made a promise to the inhabitants of Megalopolis in Arcadia that he would build a wall for them around their city. He started construction of a magnificent theater of marble for the citizens of Tegea. At Cyzicus he presented a golden table service to be used in the city's stateroom where dignitaries dined on special occasions. To the Rhodians he

16. Diodorus Siculus *Library of History* 29.32.
17. S. R. Driver, *The Book of Daniel*, in The Cambridge Bible for Schools and Colleges, p. xxxix.
18. Polybius *Histories* 28.17.
19. Edwyn R. Bevan, 2.139 n.

distributed presents of various kinds. He planned to build for the citizens of Antioch a temple of Jupiter Capitolinus whose interior would be completely covered with gold plate. He may have completed it, for Ammianus Marcellinus speaks of a "splendid temple of the Daphnaean Apollo, which that hot-tempered and cruel king Antiochus Epiphanes had built."[20] He contributed lavishly toward the construction of the temple of Zeus Olympian in Athens. Strabo says that King Antiochus dedicated this temple; however, death took him before he could complete it.[21] He beautified Delos with altars of extraordinary beauty and presented them with an abundance of Greek statues.[22] Toward the end of his life, the writer of Maccabees observes, "He now saw with alarm that he might be short of money . . . for the gifts he had been accustomed to distribute with an even more lavish hand than any of his predecessors on the throne" (1 Macc 3:30).

In his vision Daniel indicates that the Antichrist also will be lavish in his gifts to others, apparently to secure their loyalty. In particular, he will divide up the land of Israel and parcel it out to his followers. "And he shall deal with the strongest fortresses by the help of a foreign god: whosoever acknowledgeth him he will increase with glory; and he shall cause them to rule over many, and shall divide the land for a price" (Dan 11:39). "The land was not so much sold as given in return for services," observes Montgomery.[23]

The prophet Joel indicates that the Battle of Armageddon will be, in part, a punishment for a similar sacrilege committed by the Antichrist. "I will gather all nations, and will bring them down into the valley of Jehoshaphat; and I will execute judgment upon them there for my people and for my heritage Israel, whom they have scattered among the nations: and they have parted my land" (Joel 3:2).

20. Ammianus Marcellinus 22.13.1.
21. Strabo *Geography* 9.1.19.
22. Livy *The History of Rome* 41.20.
23. Montgomery, p. 463.

The relationship between the Jews and the land is unique and crucial. It has a dynamic quality that exists between no other people and their homeland. Eretz Israel, the land of Israel, was given to the Jews as a part of the original covenant which God made with Abraham (Gen 12:1-3, 7). Since it was to be their possession forever (13:15), the only time that they would legitimately forfeit it was through disobedience (Deut 28:63). However, Israel will inevitably be restored to the land (30:3-5), and there, in the land, Israel will know the Messianic blessings which are to come upon the nation in the last days (Ezek 36:24-31).

However, the Antichrist will tamper with this unique and divinely determined relationship between the people of Israel and the land of Israel by taking the land from them and giving it to others. But the Jew and the land are inviolable, and the Antichrist will be punished at Armageddon for this specific travesty, says the prophet Joel.

These are the means by which Antiochus IV Epiphanes secured the throne.

One of Israel's greatest religious leaders, Onias III, was eliminated. He was to Jerusalem what Savonarola was to Florence during the evil reign of Pope Alexander VI. Both men were popular preachers of righteousness whose rulers finally deposed them. They were both murdered. However, Onias's followers, the Hasidim, remained, emerging later to support the revolution which broke the yoke of Antiochus upon the Jews.

Hellenism, supported by a powerful few in Jerusalem, weakened the Jews for the moment by relieving Judaism of its official will to resist. For a few years King Antiochus maintained his control over the Jews because of this weakness. However, they were soon to revive their militant orthodoxy, and, opposing their Hellenistic countrymen, the Orthodox overthrew them and greatly relieved Judaism of one of the most serious threats it would face until the end days.

The allegiance of others was bought by the king, ostensibly by using the Holy Land as a means to bribe his adversaries into submission. However, Antiochus IV Epiphanes could not and the Antichrist will not be able to violate the land with impunity. The latter's throne will see collapse as a result of this and other desecrations, just as did the former's.

Antiochus IV Epiphanes' stratagems prevailed for a while. However, they failed to guarantee his control of the land. A few years later all was lost when the Jewish people rose up in righteous revolt against this evil Seleucid king.

5

Antiochus's First Egyptian Campaign and Its Aftermath

Daniel 11:25-28

Fulfilled: 169 B.C.

ANTIOCHUS IV EPIPHANES' SISTER, Cleopatra, was married to the Egyptian king, Ptolemy V Epiphanes. He died in 180 B.C. and she in 173 B.C., leaving as heir to the throne of Egypt, Ptolemy VI Philometor, a minor and a nephew of King Antiochus.

At this point in history the ownership of Coele-Syria came under dispute. A war party in Egypt, led by two of the king's regents, Eulaeus and Lenaeus, claimed that Coele-Syria belonged to Egypt because the original Ptolemy, a Diodachi, had taken possession of it after the death of Alexander the Great. Furthermore, when Antiochus III the Great gave his daughter, Cleopatra, to wed the Egyptian king, Coele-Syria was a part of her dowry. Now this youthful pharaoh, Ptolemy VI Philometor, was being pressed by his advisers, Eulaeus and Lenaeus, to invade Syria in order to reassert Egypt's claim by military force. Antiochus soon got wind of what was happening. Diodorus Siculus says, "Ptolemy, king of Egypt, knowing that his ancestors had held Coele-Syria, made great preparations for war in support of his claim, hoping that since it had been detached in times past through an unjust war he might now justly recover it on the same terms."[1]

1. Diodorus Siculus *Library of History* 30.2.

But when Ptolemy VI Philometor attempted to march out of Egypt, Antiochus IV Epiphanes marched in and met the Egyptian army before it could cross the desert which separates Egypt from Syria. Defeating Ptolemy's forces, King Antiochus occupied the frontier fortress at Pelusium. When the news of the defeat of the Egyptian army at Pelusium reached Alexandria, the young king's advisers persuaded him to flee the city by sea. However, Antiochus was fortunate enough to capture him. He then moved up the Nile River to Memphis and there, according to Porphyry, Antiochus had himself crowned king.[2] The Apocrypha confirms this, saying that Antiochus "made up his mind to become king of Egypt and so to rule over both kingdoms" (1 Macc 1:16).

It is difficult to see how the Syrian king would take such a step, for it would surely antagonize the Romans if the houses of Seleucus and Ptolemy were to unite. However, the temptation to have the ancient and mystical rites of the pharaohs conferred upon him may have been too much for Antiochus. Perhaps he had some notion of becoming another Alexander the Great and of conquering the world when he invaded Egypt. Learsi says, "The plans of conquest with which Antiochus fed his vainglory began with Egypt and were calculated to end with Rome."[3] Since he intended challenging Rome anyhow, to accept Egypt's crown was but a step in that direction.

When the boy king, Ptolemy VI Philometor, was captured by King Antiochus, the latter proposed a protectorate which would unite the two royal houses, joining Egypt and Syria and thus creating one united power in the Hellenistic east. However, the people of Alexandria revolted when they heard this, and they crowned Philometor's younger brother as king in his

2. Gleason L. Archer, trans., *Jerome's Commentary on Daniel*, p. 131; cf. W. W. Tarn, *The Greeks in Bactria and India*, p. 192.
3. Rufus Learsi, *Israel: A History of the Jewish People*, p. 130.

place. Then Egypt had two kings, Ptolemy VI Philometor, who was reigning in Memphis under the protection of Antiochus Epiphanes; and Ptolemy Euergetes, who was reigning in Alexandria. Both kings were minors and under the control of regents.

Antiochus IV Epiphanes returned home in triumph. With two rival kings in Egypt, the entire country was at his mercy.

DANIEL PREDICTS ANTIOCHUS'S INVASION OF EGYPT

And he shall stir up his power and his courage against the king of the south with a great army; and the king of the south shall war in battle with an exceeding great and mighty army; but he shall not stand; for they shall devise devices against him . . . and his army shall overflow; and many shall fall down slain. And as for both these kings, their hearts shall be to do mischief, and they shall speak lies at one table: but it shall not prosper; for yet the end shall be at the time appointed (Dan 11:25-27).

Daniel prophesied the overthrow of the king of the south, Ptolemy VI Philometor, by two means: military defeat and deception. The military defeat was most spectacular because no army had penetrated the border defenses of Egypt for 163 years. Many great generals had tried what Antiochus IV Epiphanes attempted but failed. Even Antiochus III the Great had been defeated here. But the forces of Antiochus successfully breached Egypt's border defenses.

Daniel saw Antiochus IV Epiphanes, with an exceedingly great and mighty army, invading Egypt. First Maccabees describes this army in terms of a powerful force composed of chariots, elephants, cavalry, and a great fleet (1 Macc 1:17). Hannibal of Carthage (218-202 B.C.) had used elephants against the Romans. After the Battle of Magnesia, the Romans forbade the Syrians the military use of these large animals. Nevertheless, Antiochus brought them against the Egyptians. His generals were later to use them against the Jews during the

Maccabean revolt (1 Macc 6:30). In fact, it was an elephant which killed Eleazer, one of the Maccabees, at the Battle of Beth Zur a few years later (1 Macc 6:46). Daniel also saw the battlefield carnage—"many shall fall down slain" (Dan 11:26b) —which is also mentioned in the Apocrypha, "leaving many dead" (1 Macc 1:18). Perhaps there was a threat of an unprecedented carnage at this battle. The secular historians indicate that King Antiochus endeared himself to the Egyptians by riding out among the fallen and forbidding his soldiers to kill anymore.

These words in the Apocrypha are written history. The words of Daniel are written prophecy. First Maccabees was written after the event. Daniel, however, was written over 350 years before, predicting Antiochus's battle on the Egyptian frontier in 169 B.C. with great accuracy.

The second means utilized by King Antiochus for the overthrow of the Egyptian king was deception. "They shall devise devices against him, says Daniel, "Yea, they that eat of his dainties shall destroy him" (Dan 11:25b-26).

Apparently this deception was twofold. The youthful, and possibly naive, king was tricked by his wily uncle, Antiochus. At the same time he was also misled by the members of his own court, particularly his guileful regents, Eulaeus and Lenaeus. Their deception began when they advised the young pharaoh to assert Egypt's claim on Coele-Syria by military force, for they assured him that he could easily recover Egypt's lost territories in Syria.[4] Professor Zeitlin suggests that Ptolemy Philometor also was deceived into fleeing Alexandria in advance of the invading armies of King Antiochus by this insidious pair. "The child-king Ptolemy VI may have been badly advised by his regents or, perhaps it was an act of treachery on their part to have him flee Alexandria by sea to the sacred

4. S. R. Driver, *The Book of Daniel* in The Cambridge Bible for Schools and Colleges, p. 178.

island of Samothrace, for he was intercepted there by Antiochus."[5]

However, Ptolemy VI Philometor must have been greatly deceived by his uncle, Antiochus IV Epiphanes. Porphyry suggests this, for he is quoted by Jerome as saying,

> But the king of the south, that is the generals of Ptolemy, were also roused to war with many and very powerful auxilary forces, but they could not stand against the fraudulent schemes of Antiochus. For he pretended to be at peace with his sister's son and ate bread with him, and afterward he took possession of Egypt.[6]

Polybius says that Antiochus's use of deception to gain the surrender of the Pelusium fortress was despicable.[7] The fact that King Antiochus championed the claim of Ptolemy Philometor over that of his younger brother whom the Alexanderenes had crowned king, is further evidence of his hypocrisy, for he was not interested in securing his nephew Philometor upon the throne, but in furthering his own interests in Egypt.

In 11:27, Daniel represents "both these kings"—Ptolemy VI Philometor and his uncle, Antiochus IV Epiphanes—sitting at the same table telling each other lies. Undoubtedly Antiochus insisted that his only interest in the conquest of Egypt was to secure its throne for his nephew, while his nephew circumvented a crisis by pretending a belief in his uncle's assurances. The whole Egyptian affair was wrapped in an aura of intrigue and deception that was apparent to everyone, but it was conveniently ignored at the court of Memphis while the king of Syria and his nephew, the king of Egypt, feigned mutual trust in each other.

Antiochus's fraudulent behavior in Egypt was consistent with what we know of his character. It also typifies the Antichrist, who is characterized in Scripture as an arch-deceiver.

5. Solomon Zeitlin, *The Rise and Fall of the Judean State*, 1:86.
6. Archer, p. 132.
7. Polybius *Histories* 27.18.

"And through his policy he shall cause craft to prosper in his hand" (Dan 8:25), "even he, whose coming is according to the working of Satan with all power and signs and lying wonders, and with all deceit of unrighteousness for them that perish; because they received not the love of the truth, that they might be saved. And for this cause God sendeth them a working of error, that they should believe a lie: that they all might be judged who believed not the truth, but had pleasure in unrighteousness" (2 Thess 2:9-12), " and there was given to him a mouth speaking great things and blasphemies" (Rev 13:5).

The deceit of the Antichrist will be similar to that of Antiochus, for he will simulate an interest in the plight of all mankind in a world made chaotic by war, famine, and pestilence (Rev 6:1-4). In the last days he will rise as a benevolent dictator who is dedicated to redressing the world's ills. At that time a recent event—the sudden disappearance of all Christians—will severely shake the world's religious, political, and economic structure. Such a strong man will be needed to take over the leadership of international affairs. The dramatic and reassuring words of the Antichrist will indicate that he is the man.

At first he will solve the pressing problems of world need. However, three and one half years after he takes over the reign of world government, his true intents will be revealed. He will have deceived mankind into thinking that he is a concerned autocrat who is willing to devote his genius to the solution of world problems and to the betterment of world conditions. But then the awesome truth will emerge that he is an evil demagogue who is determined to be worshiped as God.

ANTIOCHUS'S TERROR IN JERUSALEM

Then shall he return into his land with great substance; and his heart shall be against the holy covenant; and he shall do his pleasure, and return to his own land (Dan 11:28).

On his way down into Egypt, Antiochus had visited Jerusalem (2 Macc 4:21-22), where he was given a brilliant welcome with a torchlight parade and other ovations befitting a visiting monarch. Though this may not have represented the popular feeling, it certainly suited the pro-Seleucid Jews, for this lavish reception was arranged and promoted by Jason, the hellenizing high priest.

Leaving Egypt after his first invasion and victory there, Antiochus visited Jerusalem again on his way back to his own capital, Antioch. That time his reception was far different, for he came in terror to loot, burn, and massacre.

The chronology of Antiochus's visits to Egypt is unsure. Scholars are not certain if he invaded Egypt two or three times. Daniel indicates two invasions. Furthermore, the time of Antiochus's violation of the Temple in Jerusalem is also uncertain. First Maccabees (1:20-28) has it taking place after the first invasion, while 2 Maccabees (5:15-21) places it after the second invasion.[8]

The reason for the sacrilege and massacre is also in dispute. Did Antiochus want money? Was this the reason for his robbing the Temple of its treasure? There is no doubt that his brother, Seleucis IV Philopator, and his father, Antiochus III the Great, robbed temples for this reason. However, both Daniel and 1 Maccabees (1:19) indicate that he was then rich with spoil from Egypt. In addition, there is some evidence that Antiochus distributed the Temple treasure to other cities in his empire as presents. Perhaps it was the rumor of his death which had caused an uprising in Jerusalem that made him feel he had to punish the Jews after his victory over Egypt. Or did the rumor not circulate until his second invasion of Egypt? We are unsure.

8. John R. Bartlett, *The First and Second Books of the Maccabees*, p. 24.

Since much is uncertain here, we will follow Professor Zeit-lin's chronology as a means of bringing some order to these events. He maintains that Antiochus's violation of the Temple occurred after the first invasion of Egypt, and that the attending massacre was retaliation for Judea's attempt to deny him access to the Temple's sacred precincts. In addition, the rumor of the king's death, with its resulting uprising in Jerusalem, did not occur until Antiochus's second invasion of Egypt.[9]

First Maccabees records the events which took place when Antiochus IV Epiphanes visited Jerusalem after his first and victorious campaign in Egypt against the king of the south in 169 B.C.

> On his return from the conquest of Egypt, in the year 143 [i.e., 169 B.C.], Antiochus marched with a strong force against Israel and Jerusalem. In his arrogance he entered the temple and carried off the golden altar, the lamp-stand with all its equipment, the table for the Bread of the Presence, the sacred cups and bowls, the golden censers, the curtain, and the crowns. He stripped off all the gold plating from the temple front. He seized the silver, gold, and precious vessels, and whatever secret treasures he found, and took them all with him when he left for his own country. He had caused much bloodshed, and he gloated over all he had done (1 Macc 1:20-24).

Since Jerusalem had become a Greek city, "Antioch-Jerusalem," by previous decree of the emperor, he no doubt felt that he had the right to visit the Temple in spite of his father's long-standing assurance that no Gentile could enter contrary to Jewish tradition.

And so Antiochus entered the Temple, penetrating the Holy of Holies where the Law of God declared that only the high priest could go, once a year. Rumors spread about what he found there. These rumors were to bring the Jews into disrepute among the civilized nations, for the repercussions

9. Zeitlin, 1:86.

from them were felt particularly in the Middle Ages, and even down to our own day. Antiochus spread the report that upon entering the Holy of Holies he found the stone image of a man with a long beard sitting upon a donkey, holding a book in his hand. The king interpreted the figure to be Moses, the giver of the Law. However, it was the story of the donkey on which he sat that made a lasting impression, for, from that time on, the Greeks and Romans believed that the Jews worshiped an ass.

Antiochus was probably guilty of another lie which has maligned the Jewish people from that day until recently. It was rumored that he found a Greek imprisoned in the Temple, lying on a bed. This Greek pleaded wth Antiochus to set him free, for, said he, the Jews were feeding him in order to prepare him for a ritual sacrifice in which he would be killed and his intestines eaten. During this ceremony the Jews were supposedly to take an oath of hatred for all Greeks. As a result, the notion spread that the Jewish religion included hatred for all nations.

The idea of the ritual sacrifice of a human being by the Jews persisted until it caused much suspicion of the Jewish community during the Middle Ages and even into the twentieth century. Elie Wiesel's novel *The Oath* is built upon this theme. The origin of these atrocious stories goes back to the time of Antiochus.

When King Antiochus left the Temple, he took with him the sacred vessels, furniture, and other items of value. First Maccabees 1:21-24 lists the treasures and the sacred furniture used in the Temple services which the king took away. However, this was not the first time, or the last, that the Temple was robbed of its furnishings. Nebuchadnezzar had carried the original furnishings into Babylon. After the Great Revolt, Titus took similar furnishings to Rome. But in 169 B.C. Antiochus took them to Antioch.

This indicates that the menorah, the table of shewbread,

and the altar of incense which occupied the holy place in the original tabernacle in the wilderness and in the first Temple are long since lost. Duplicates were made according to the pattern given in Exodus 25-27. Apparently this is how the Temple's holy place was refurnished after the reclamation of the Temple in 165 B.C. (1 Macc 4:49).

One piece of furniture, the Ark of the Covenant, was never reproduced. Antiochus IV Epiphanes did not desecrate the Ark, for it was absent from the Holy of Holies in the second Temple. Tradition has it that Jeremiah hid the Ark of the Covenant before Nebuchadnezzar could capture the Temple in 587 B.C. (2 Macc 2:1-6).

But what about the Ark of the Covenant? Perhaps the original will yet be recovered from its hiding place. Various traditions exist about its fate. The Apocrypha, as we have noted, says that Jeremiah took it to Mount Nebo where it was deposited in a cave. The location of this cave was not marked. Jeremiah said, "The place shall remain unknown . . . until God finally gathers his people together and shows mercy to them (2 Macc 2:7). Another legend says that it was hidden under the floor of the wood-storage room in the Temple. One day a priest discovered its resting place and was struck dead when he was about to reveal its location to others. Another story says Solomon knew that the Temple which he built would be destroyed. Therefore he made a trapdoor under the Holy of Holies through which the Ark could fall to safety, deep in the earth under Temple Mount. *The Syriac Apocalypse of Baruch* describes an angel coming to the Temple when it was engulfed in flames to rescue the Ark. He then commits it to the earth for safekeeping:

> Earth! earth! earth! Hear the word of the mighty God,
> And receive what I commit to thee,
> And guard them until the last times,
> So that strangers may not get possession of them.

> For the time comes when Jerusalem also will be delivered
> for a time.
> Until it is said, that it is again restored forever.

And the earth opened its mouth and swallowed up the Ark.[10]
All of these legends come to the same conclusion, suggesting that there is some substance behind these stories. The original Ark of the Covenant which was made for the tabernacle in the wilderness, and which later disappeared from the first Temple, has never been found. The Jews felt free to reproduce the furniture for the holy Place: the menorah, the table of shewbread, and the altar of incense, each time the Temple was robbed. But they never felt free to reproduce the Ark of the Covenant with the Mercy Seat above. This is why it did not appear in the second Temple after the Exile. However, the original which disappeared when the first Temple fell may still be hidden in Israel, ready to be revealed and used in the Temple during the Messianic era.

We are relatively sure about what happened to one treasure which Antiochus IV Epiphanes took from the Temple, the veil which separated the holy place from the Holy of Holies. It is a matter of record that King Antiochus presented to the Zeus temple in Olympia a remarkable curtain of beautiful workmanship, embroidered and interwoven with figures. Where did he get it? Pausanias, the Greek doctor who spent several years traveling about Greece in the second century A.D., recording in detail everything that he saw in each Greek city and sanctuary, speculates that the curtain in the Olympia temple was the same curtain which King Antiochus took from the Temple in Jerusalem and presented to the Zeus temple.[11] Some scholars admit the plausibility of Pausanias's theory.

> There is some grounds for believing that this Eastern curtain, presented to the Temple of Zeus by Antiochus, had

10. 2 Baruch 6:1 ff. in R. H. Charles, *The Apocrypha and Pseudepigrapha of the Old Testament*, 2:483-84.
11. Pausanias *Guide to Greece* 5.12.4.

been originally the Veil of the Temple in Jerusalem. For
Antiochus carried off the Veil (I Macc 1:22; *Ant.,* XII.5.4)
and after robbing and defiling the Temple, attempted to re-
consecrate it to Olympian Zeus (II Macc. 6:2). It would be
very natural that Antiochus should dedicate to Zeus in the
most famous of his sanctuaries the curtain which he had
carried off from the Temple at Jerusalem.[12]

Ganneau says,

> I even venture to ask whether the veil of the Olympian
> Temple might not have been the very veil of the Temple of
> Jerusalem carried off by Antiochus IV, the great pillager of
> Temples. . . . To whom did Antiochus dedicate the Temple
> of Jerusalem plundered and defiled by him? To Olympian
> Zeus (2 Macc 6:2). We need not be astonished, therefore,
> if he hung up the veil of the Jewish Temple in that of
> Olympian Zeus. Are not always the spoils of the conquered
> deity consecrated to the victorious deity?[13]

However, Antiochus's treachery in robbing the Temple at
that time was a mild sacrilege compared to what he would do
a year so so later when he again visited Jerusalem after his
second invasion of Egypt.

In his terrorizing visit to Jerusalem in 169 b.c., Antiochus
not only desecrated the Temple by robbing it of its furnishings, but he also murdered a large number of Jews in Jerusalem.

> He had caused much bloodshed, and he gloated over all
> he had done.

> Great was the lamentation throughout Israel;
> rulers and elders groaned in bitter grief.
> Girls and young men languished;
> the beauty of our women was disfigured.
> Every bridegroom took up the lament,

12. J. G. Frazer, *Pausanias' Description of Greece,* 3:545-46.
13. C. Clermont Ganneau, "The Veil of the Temple of Jerusalem at Olympia," in *The Palestine Exploration Fund: Quarterly Statement for 1878,*
p. 241.

and every bride sat grieving in her chamber.
The land trembled for its inhabitants,
and all the house of Jacob was wrapped in shame.

1 MACCABEES 1:24-28

The destruction of the first Temple in 587 B.C. evoked the writing of the book of Lamentations. After the second Temple fell in A.D. 70 the rabbis reapplied the words of Lamentations, in Midrashic form, to the aftermath of the Great Revolt. Here the writer of 1 Maccabees follows this same pattern, for his words are a song of lament for the desecrated Temple and the massacred people. He issued a similar lament when Antiochus repeated this desecration of the Temple and a massacre a year so later (1 Macc 1:37-40; cf. 2:7-11; 3:45).

The fate of the Temple and the security of the people hang together here, as they always do in Jewish literature. When the Temple falls, the people are massacred and disbursed. The security of the people in the land seems irrevocably bound by a mystical link to the Temple itself. This is one reason why we believe that the Temple must be rebuilt when Israel enters a time of security during the first years of the Antichrist's reign. This is also why a permanent Temple will be established in the Messianic reign of Israel's peace.

When the Six-Day War ended, Elie Wiesel wrote:

> The crowd keeps getting larger. Military personnel and officials, celebrities and journalists, all are streaming by in one continuous procession, along with rabbis and students, gathered from all over the city, from every corner of the land. Men, women and adolescents of every age, every origin and speaking every language, and I see these ascending toward the Wall, toward all that remains of their collective longing.[14]

Legend says that when the Temple was destroyed by Titus in A.D. 70, a half dozen angels sat atop the wall, weeping for

14. Elie Wiesel, *A Beggar in Jerusalem*, p. 241.

the lost Temple. Their tears soaked into the very stones and so toughened the mortar that the wall stands forever, even today, and beyond time.

Another legend says that every night heaven weeps for the lost Temple. Those tears can be seen on the wall each morning (skeptics would say that this was dew collected there by night!).

In addition to this mystical link between the security of the people and the inviolability of the Temple, there is another principle which appears in Jewish history—the one who violates the Temple will not long prosper.

The destruction of those who desecrate the Temple of the Lord in Jerusalem is a well-established literary device among the ancient writers as well as a fact of history. The fate of Sennacherib seems to serve as the literary and theological framework for this poetic justice (2 Kings 18:17—19:37). During the reign of the Seleucid king, Demetrius, General Nicanor was sent to Jerusalem to capture Judas Maccabee. He threatened to burn the Temple. For his blasphemy, Nicanor was slain in battle (1 Macc 7:26-43; cf. 2 Macc 14:33—15:27).

Titus, Vespasian's son, was in command of the Roman forces surrounding Jerusalem when the city fell in A.D. 70. The Romans were unable to break through the walls which surrounded the Temple Mount when a soldier cast a burning torch into the Temple and it immediately burst into flames. When entrance was gained into the area, Titus had the flames extinguished. He entered the Holy of Holies, accompanied by two Jewish prostitutes. Spreading the scroll of the Law out on the floor, he desecrated it. Then, with his sword, he slashed the veil which separated the Holy of Holies from the rest of the sanctuary. As if by a miracle, says Jewish legend, blood flowed out and Titus laughed, saying, "I have killed the God of the Jews!" The proud general then took down the curtain and used it for a basket in which to carry off the vessels of the

Temple. They were placed on board ship and Titus sailed off to Rome in triumph.

While at sea, a mighty storm broke. Titus said, "It seems that the strength of the God of Israel lies in the waters. Pharaoh, king of Egypt, he drowned in water. Sisera, the mighty general, he also drowned by means of water and me too he also desires to drown in water. If he is a hero, let him come up to dry land and there engage with me in battle!"

Whereupon a heavenly voice was heard to say, "O thou son of the wicked and great grandson of Esau the wicked! I have an unimportant creature in my world called a 'gnat.' Go on dry land and engage in combat with it."

When Titus's feet touched land, a little gnat entered his nose. This small creature bored into his brain for the next seven years, causing unbearable pain.

One day Titus passed a blacksmith who was pounding with a hammer on an anvil. At the sound of the hammer, the gnat grew quiet. Every day thereafter Titus had a blacksmith come to him and beat with a hammer upon an anvil in order to still the gnat. If the blacksmith were a pagan, he would pay him four zuzim per day, but if he were a Jew, Titus would pay him nothing, saying, "You have sufficient reward for your work, when you see your arch-enemy suffer thus."

This remedy was effective only for thirty days. After this the gnat became used to the hammer and began gnawing again.

When Titus was about to die, he said, "Burn my corpse and scatter the ashes of it upon the seven seas so that the God of the Jews shall be unable to find me and put me on trial for my cruel deeds."

When Titus was dead, so the legend goes, his head was opened and in his skull was found a gnat the size of a bird. Its beak was of copper and its talons of iron.[15]

Polybius records that his contemporaries believed that An-

15. Hyman E. Golden, *The Book of Legends*, 3:159-61.

tiochus IV Epiphanes received divine judgment for similar
Temple desecration. "He died at Tabae in Persia, smitten
with madness, as some people say, owning to certain manifestations of divine displeasure when he was attempting this out-
rage on the above sanctuary.[16] In this case it was a pagan sanctuary. However, the Jews also felt that Antiochus came to his
untimely death under the judgment of God.

> When the king heard this news [King Antiochus learned of
> the success of the Maccabean revolt], he was thrown into
> such deep dismay that he took to his bed, ill with grief at
> the miscarriage of his plans. There he lay for many days, his
> bitter grief breaking out again and again, and he realized
> that he was dying. So he summoned all his Friends and said
> to them: 'Sleep has deserted me; the weight of care has
> broken my heart. At first I said to myself, "Why am I over-
> whelmed by this flood of trouble, I who was kind and well-
> loved in the day of my power?" But now I remember the
> wrong I did in Jerusalem, when I took all her vessels of silver
> and gold, and when I made an unjustified attempt to wipe
> out the inhabitants of Judaea. It is for this, I know, that
> these misfortunes have come upon me; and here I am, dying
> of grief in a foreign land.' (1 Macc 6:8-13; cf. 2 Macc 1:13-17;
> 9:1-29).

16. Polybius, 31.9.

6

The Day of Eleusis

Daniel 11:29-30

Fulfilled: 168 B.C.

MORE THAN A HUNDRED YEARS after the death of Antiochus IV Epiphanes, Cicero, the Roman orator, stood in the Senate in Rome to speak. The date was February 43 B.C. In his speech he lamented that the Romans had lost the spirit of their fathers, that aggressiveness which halted King Antiochus in Egypt. Said Cicero:

> When in the days of our ancestors Gaius Popillius had been sent as envoy to King Antiochus and had in the words of the Senate ordered him to retire from Alexandria which he was besieging, the King began to waste time, and Popillius drew a line round him as he stood, and said he would report him to the Senate if the King did not reply what his intentions were before he stepped out of that circle. A noble action! for he had brought with him the personification of the Senate and the authority of the Roman people.[1]

This event, which Cicero recalled for the Roman Senate before whom he spoke, has been named "The Day of Eleusis." It is one of the most famous confrontations in all ancient history. The Day of Eleusis is noted by many of the secular historians of the ancient world: Polybius (*The Histories* 29.27) ; Livy (*History of Rome* 45.12.3-6) ; Diodorus Siculus (*Library of History* 31.2) ; Velleius (*Historiae Romanae* 1.10.1) ; Valerius Maximus (*Nine Books* 6.4.3.) ; Appian (*Syriaca* 66) ;

1. Cicero *Philippic* 8.23; cf. Justinius *History of the World* 34.3.1-4.

Justinius (*History of the World* 34.3.1-4) ; Josephus (*Antiquities* 12.5.2.).

It was also forecast by Daniel the prophet, who said that the ships of Kittim would come against Antiochus IV Epiphanes to force him to return to his own land.

It came about like this:

ANTIOCHUS'S SECOND INVASION OF EGYPT

> At the time appointed he shall return, and come into the south; but it shall not be in the latter time as it was in the former. For ships of Kittim shall come against him; therefore he shall be grieved, and shall return (Dan 11:29-30*a*).

Antiochus IV Epiphanes had withdrawn from Egypt just a year earlier, leaving the country divided under the rule of two different kings. However, it was not long before these two kings agreed to unite. Ptolemy Philometor returned to Alexandria, where he and his brother, Ptolemy Euergetes, became joint rulers of Egypt.

Antiochus faced a dilemma. He had to put down this unified threat to his sovereignty. However, his position was rather awkward, for he had proclaimed to the Greek world that his previous invasion of Egypt was to establish his nephew, the legitimate king, on the throne. His first invasion of Egypt was also justified by Egypt's threat of aggression toward his own territory. The Greek world had sanctioned Antiochus's first invasion. Furthermore, the Romans had been too busy fighting in Macedonia to do anything about it.

But this time Antiochus was interfering in what was a purely internal matter. Letters detailing the reasons for the first invasion of Egypt were in the archives of numerous cities. However, "forgetful of all that he had written and said, Antiochus began preparing for a renewal of the war against Ptolemy," says Polybius.[2]

2. Polybius *Histories* 29.26.

As Antiochus moved south along the desert road between Palestine and Egypt, he met envoys of Ptolemy VI Philometor. After politely thanking him for his previous aid in securing the legitimate king of Egypt on the throne of his fathers, they remonstrated with him for his present warlike aggression. Antiochus issued an ultimatum demanding the formal cession of Cyprus and Pelusium within a fixed period. From these two points King Antiochus could control Egypt; Pelusium by land and Cyprus by sea. When the deadline was passed, the Syrian king invaded Egypt for a second time and marched to Memphis. From Memphis he turned north with Alexandria in his sights.

And then it happened—the Day of Eleusis—a day so traumatic in the career of Antiochus IV Epiphanes that many believe that he was irretrievably shaken by it, and, as a result, he became the malevolent monster who is remembered in history as one of the most evil persecutors the Jews would ever encounter until the time of the Antichrist, whom Antiochus prefigured.

Prior to this time the forces of Rome had been engaged in subduing the Macedonian states, so the rising empire could give little attention to events in Egypt. But on June 22, 168 B.C. Macedonia fell forever into the Roman pale. Now the Senate was free to consider the balance of power which Antiochus was disturbing in the east by his invasion of Egypt. He must be stopped. They dispatched an envoy, General Gaius Popillius Laenas, with specific instructions for King Antiochus.

Antiochus's army was even then in the suburbs of Alexandria, camped at a place called Eleusis.

Diodorus Siculus gives an account of the following event:

> As the Romans approached, Antiochus, after greeting them verbally from a distance, stretched out his hand in welcome. Popillius, however, who had in readiness the document in which the senate's decree was recorded, held it out and

ordered Antiochus to read it. His purpose in acting thus, it was thought, was that he might avoid clasping the king's hand in friendship until it was evident from his decision whether he was, in fact, friend or foe. When the king, after reading the document, said that he would consult with his friends on these matters, Popillius, hearing this, acted in a manner that seemed offensive and arrogant in the extreme. Having a vinestock ready in his hand, with the stick he drew a line about Antiochus, and directed him to give his answer in that circle. The king, astonished by what had taken place, and awed, too, by the majesty and might of Rome, found himself in a hopeless quandary, and on full consideration said that he would do all that the Romans proposed. Popillius and his colleagues then took his hand and greeted him cordially.[3]

Polybius says, "The contents of the despatch was an order to end the war with Ptolemy at once. Accordingly a stated number of days were allowed him, within which he withdrew his army into Syria, in high dudgeon indeed, and groaning in spirit, but yielding to the necessities of the time."[4]

Daniel predicted this event, using the figure of the coming of the "ships of Kittim" (11:30). "Kittim" is used in the Old Testament as a general designation for the peoples of the Mediterranean world, especially Cyprus. Josephus says, "From it [Cyprus] all the islands and most of the parts beyond the seas are called Kittim by the Hebrews."[5] In 1 Maccabees (1: 1; 8:5) "Kittim" is used in reference to Macedonia. But here in Daniel's prophecy it is used in reference to the Romans.

Some of the rabbis believed that Baalam had predicted the Day of Eleusis centuries before. He used the same figure when he prophesied:

> But ships shall come from the
> coast of Kittim,

3. Diodorus Siculus *Library of History* 31.2.
4. Polybius, 29.27.
5. Josephus *Antiquities* 1.6.1.

> And they shall afflict Asshur,
> and shall afflict Eber;
> And he also shall come to
> destruction.

NUMBERS 24:24

In Baalam's prophecy Kittim is identified as the Romans by the Rabbis Rashi and Nachmanides.[6] The Romans will come, predicted Baalam, over a thousand years before the event, and shall afflict Assur (Syria) and Eber (the Jews), and he also (Antiochus) shall come to destruction.

We have previously noted Antiochus's erratic behavior. Soon after the Day of Eleusis, Antiochus's entire personality seemed to degenerate. Professor Tarn says, "Many believe that Antiochus's character showed marked alteration after the Day of Eleusis."[7] King Antiochus was always pushed by an inordinate aggression which was neurotic. But then, his aggression was accompanied by an attitude toward the Jews which was psychotic. He died just a few years later in Parthia, a victim of "consumption of the lungs."[8] Since tuberculosis was incurable in the ancient world, Professor Tarn believes that Antiochus was aware of his slow death as a consumptive and that this accounts for the "nervous haste" which characterized his reign.[9] Knowing that he was doomed, he wanted to accomplish as much as possible before the end came. In his later years, however, his neurosis was further compounded by his rebuff and subsequent hatred for the Romans. Since he could not vent his pent-up fury upon Rome, he released it upon the Jews.

Antiochus IV Epiphanes, in obedience to the Roman Senate's edict, left Egypt.

---

6. A. Cohen, *The Soncino Chumash*, p. 928; cf. James A. Montgomery, *A Critical and Exegetical Commentary on the Book of Daniel*, p. 183.
7. W. W. Tarn, *The Greeks in Bactria and India*, p. 183.
8. Polybius, 31.9.11; Appian *The Syrian Wars* 66; cf. 1 Macc 1:12; 2 Macc 9:1 ff.
9. Tarn, p. 215.

During one of his visits to Egypt, a rumor circulated that the king had been killed. The news of his death caused a civil uprising in Jerusalem. Did this rumor occur during Antiochus's first or his second invasion of Egypt? If the latter is the case, as we will now assume, then another question arises: Did Antiochus also visit Jerusalem after his second invasion of Egypt after the Day of Eleusis had occurred?

"His discomfiture in connection with the ultimatum of Popillius started a rumor that he had died," says Professor Zeitlin,[10] indicating his belief that the famous rumor about the king's death circulated *after* Antiochus's second invasion of Egypt. The effect which this rumor had upon Jerusalem necessitated a second punitive visit to the city by Antiochus himself on his return home to Antioch.

We are following the chronology of Zeitlin, which is the chronology of 2 Maccabees. This chronology is consistent with the book of Daniel, which also indicates two invasions of Egypt, followed by side visits to Jerusalem each time Antiochus left Egypt for Antioch.[11] The inspiration of the Holy Spirit confirms for us the integrity and the historical accuracy of Daniel. Accordingly, the prophet's chronology is normative.

When the rumor spread that Antiochus IV Epiphanes was dead, Jason, the deposed high priest who was living in exile across the Jordan in Ammonite territory, attacked Jerusalem

10. Solomon Zeitlin, *The Rise and Fall of the Judean State,* 1:87-88.
11. Victor Tcherikover also contends for two punitive visits to Jerusalem on the basis of Daniel, whom he assumes to have been a contemporary of these events (*Hellenistic Civilization of the Jews,* p. 186). An alternative view is to assume that the rumor of his death spread during the first invasion of Egypt and that he visited Jerusalem after the first invasion to rob the Temple and to massacre the people in reprisal for their revolt at hearing the news of his death. After his second invasion of Egypt, Antiochus returned to Antioch without visiting Jerusalem, and instead he sent his representatives to subdue the Jews and to attempt the hellenization of the city by force. For this position, see Edwyn R. Bevan, *The House of Seleucus,* vol. 2, chaps. 23, 25. Professor Bevan also contends for the same position in his article, "Syria and the Jews," in *The Cambridge Ancient History,* 8:505 ff.

with an army of followers (2 Macc 5:5). It is rather certain that the majority of the people in the Jewish capital preferred Jason above the Benjamite Menelaus as high priest. Menelaus was forced to take refuge in the citadel along with the Greek troops which occupied the city. Many of the pro-Selucid party of Menelaus were put to death by the followers of Jason. However, when the news reached Jerusalem that King Antiochus was not dead and was even then hastening toward the city to put down the rebellion, Jason vacated Jerusalem for the safety of Ammon, leaving his fellow Jews in the city to face the wrath of Antiochus, who was very much alive, contrary to rumor.

This would not be the only time that the Jews' optimism about the death of a tyrant would be shattered. A similar rumor will circulate in the end days about the Antichrist (Rev 13:3, 12, 14). He, too, will be reported dead. However, this rumor will also be false. The Antichrist will then come to Jerusalem to vent his fury upon the Jews, just as did his predecessor, King Antiochus in the second century B.C.[12]

ANTIOCHUS'S SECOND PUNITIVE VISIT TO JERUSALEM

Therefore he shall be grieved, and shall return, and have indignation against the holy covenant, and shall do his pleasure: he shall even return, and have regard unto them that forsake the holy covenant (Dan 11:30b).

Antiochus IV Epiphanes came back to Jerusalem, thinking that the fighting between Jason and Menelaus was actually a revolt against his authority, which it was. He stormed the city, and, once again, many Jews were massacred.

By the time Antiochus reached Jerusalem, Jason had again fled the capital and Menelaus was released from the place of his imprisonment. The fury of King Antiochus was vent upon a major portion of the people of Jerusalem who had supported

12. For a full explanation of this event, see Walter K. Price, *The Coming Antichrist*, pp. 127-28.

Jason in this struggle. This is why Daniel says that Antiochus had "regard unto them that forsake the covenant," that is, for the illegitimate Benjamite high priest, Menelaus, and his ultrahellenizing party of supporters. They were the Jewish forsakers of the covenant whom Antiochus championed at that time. They had been beaten by Jason's supporters. Then, with the aid of Antiochus, they reaped their revenge upon their fellow Jews, those helpless citizens who had been forsaken by Jason and his fighting men.

With swift and cruel action, Antiochus put down the revolt. Our sources indicate that 40,000 Jews were slain and another 40,000 sold into slavery (2 Macc 5:14). However, this one action on the part of Antiochus was not enough to insure against future uprisings. The king sent Apollonius to the city to continue his policy of oppression. Apparently by the time Apollonius could arrive, the city had stiffened its resistance once again. Apollonius had to gain entrance by deceit (1 Macc 1:29-32; 2 Macc 5:24-26).

The Acra was billeted with Greek soldiers. Many of its orthodox Jewish citizens fled, leaving Jerusalem to its predictable fate. Professor Tcherikover says that Greek and Roman history bear witness to the fact that the establishment of a colony of foreign soldiers in a town usually meant its total ruin.[13] Therefore, this event marked the beginning of an era of unprecedented, bitter, and extended persecution of the Jews.

Many scholars believe that the "Era of Anger" spoken of in the Dead Sea Scrolls culminated at this time during the reign of King Antiochus. Reference to the "Era of Anger" is found in *The Zedokite Document*. In this scroll the "Era of Anger" includes the 390 years following Jerusalem's fall in 587 B.C. Added to this was an additional twenty years in which the remnant of Israel were "like blind men groping their way.[14]

13. Abraham Schalit, ed., *The Hellenistic Age*, 6:134.
14. Theodor H. Gaster, *The Dead Sea Scriptures*, p. 61.

This brings the date for the termination of the "Era of Anger," or the "Age of Wrath" as it is otherwise translated, down to the reign of Antiochus. Other names, such as "the ring of slaughter"[15] and the time of "very great wrath upon Israel" (see 1 Macc 1:64; cf. 3:8), have been used in Jewish literature to designate the severe persecutions of King Antiochus.

The years of the Antiochus crisis are a prototype of the end days and the time of persecution which the Jews will face prior to the coming of the Messiah. Daniel calls these last days of persecution "a time of trouble, such as never was since there was a nation" (12:1). Jeremiah designates these days of intense persecution as a "time of Jacob's trouble" (Jer 30:7), while the Lord Jesus Christ calls this era one of "great tribulation" (Matt 24:21). It is interesting that many of the Talmudic rabbis themselves taught that the advent of the Messiah will be preceded by a time of great distress for Israel. They used such terms as "the birth pangs of the Messiah" and "the Messianic travail" for this era.[16]

Why do the Talmudic, Midrashic, and biblical literature view the establishment of the Messianic Kingdom as preceded by a time of unprecedented persecution for the Jews? Most Jewish writings are consistent in affirming that the final spiritual Jewish state will come about only through the purging effects of great tribulation. Much of the book of the Revelation is given to an apocalyptic description of the time of great suffering in the end days which will lead to the coming of the Messiah and to the establishment of the Kingdom on earth. Most Jewish literature, including the Bible, sustains this inspired principle: Israel, the covenant people of God, will come to know their Messiah and will enter an era of peace only through the crisis of great suffering.

Out of the Antiochus holocaust emerged the Hasmonean

15. *Sukkah* (The Babylonian Talmud, Soncino ed.) 5.8c. Cf. Martin Hengel, *Judaism and Hellenism,* 1:225.
16. Joseph Klausner, *The Messianic Idea in Israel,* pp. 440-50; Walter K. Price, *Next Year in Jerusalem,* pp. 106-35.

In the Final Days

state of Israel which became relatively peaceful, free, and independent—for a short time.

Out of the Nazi holocaust emerged the present political State of Israel. Agus says, "The state of Israel would not have taken its present form were it not for the external pressures of the Nazis."[17]

And finally, out of the Great Tribulation holocaust will emerge the new spiritual state of Israel.

THE RELEVANCE OF THE APOCALYPTIC

Thou seest the heavens, as troubled with man's act,
Threaten his bloody state. By the clock 'tis day,
And yet dark night strangles the traveling lamp.
Is't night's predominance, or the day's shame,
That darkness does the face of the earth entomb
When living light should kiss it?
Macbeth 2.4.5-9.

Thus did Ross describe the crisis days which surrounded the death of Scotland's King Duncan. They were filled with unnatural events which portended of disaster.

Just before the second Temple fell to the Romans in A.D. 70, Josephus reports a sign of this impending doom which appeared in heaven. "Before sun-setting, chariots and troops of soldiers in their armor were seen running about among the clouds, and surrounding the cities."[18] Tacitus also relates a similar vision: "Contending hosts were seen meeting in the skies, arms flashed, and suddenly the temple was illuminated with fire from the clouds."[19]

The writer of 2 Maccabees uses this same literary device to introduce Antiochus's second invasion of Jerusalem. He describes an apocalyptic apparition which all of the citizens of Jerusalem witnessed for forty days.

17. Jacob Bernard Augus, *The Meaning of Jewish History*, 1:8.
18. Josephus *Wars* 6.5.3.
19. Tacitus *Histories* 5.13.

> Apparitions were seen in the sky all over Jerusalem for nearly forty days: galloping horsemen in golden armour, companies of spearmen standing to arms, swords unsheathed, cavalry divisions in battle order. Charges and counter-charges were made on each side, shields were shaken, spears massed and javelins hurled; breastplates and golden ornaments of every kind shone brightly (2 Macc 5:2-3).

Obviously we are not dealing with inspired Scripture here. Nevertheless, these quotations do indicate the relevancy of the apocalyptic to these times of crisis. It will soon be apparent that the inspired Word utilizes the same apocalyptical approach to great periods of woe in Jewish history, such as the Antiochus crisis, the Roman crisis, and the Great Tribulation crisis.

We are not sure what the apocalyptic vision in 2 Maccabees is supposed to mean, except that Jerusalem was about to face a critical situation. As a preface to Antiochus's second visit to Jerusalem, this vision, seen in the sky, could be a good or an evil omen. Therefore the people of Jerusalem pray "that this apparition might portend good" (2 Macc 5:4). It did not, however, for King Antiochus was about to unleash one of history's most terrible pogroms upon the Jews.

This relationship between apocalyptic literature and the times of crisis is a well-established principle in the prophetic Word. The apocalyptic literature of Daniel is germane, in part at least, to the Antiochus crisis. Jesus' apocalyptic discourse (Matt 24) is directed in part to the Roman crisis of A.D. 70, while the book of the revelation is an apocalypse related to the Great Tribulation crisis which will precede the advent of the Messiah in the end days.

Each era of great stress has its apocalyptic to encourage those who are persecuted and which only the initiated can understand (Matt 24:15). The truth which the apocalypse conveys sustains those who are spiritually perceptive, while its images only confound their persecutors, the enemies of God's people.

Therefore, the Jews during the Antiochus crisis were sustained by the apocalyptic visions of Daniel. This is not to advocate a Maccabean date for the authorship of Daniel, nor does it imply that Daniel's vision is solely related to the Antiochus crisis. However, it does recognize that the material found in Daniel has profound implications for the Jews during the era leading up to, and including, the Maccabean revolt. So relevant, of course, that many modern scholars believe that the book of Daniel was actually written during this time because it reflects so clearly the events surrounding Antiochus's persecutions. Bartlett says,

> It is now generally agreed that this book was written at the height of the Maccabean struggle, shortly before the death of Antiochus. It uses stories and legends about an ancient figure called Daniel, and the literary device of the vision, to encourage men to resist Antiochus. The kingdoms of this world, including his, will soon be swept away by the arrival of God's kingdom.[20]

This is speculation. Nothing conclusive demands that we must assign the authorship of the book of Daniel to the Maccabean age. Nevertheless, we do recognize the relevancy of Daniel's material to this period in Jewish history. So did the Jews, for they could make spiritual application: the Babylonians represented the Seleucids, Nebuchadnezzar is in reality Antiochus IV Epiphanes, and the things which happened to Daniel and his friends are happening to contemporary Jews. Daniel speaks of a Babylonian king who carried off the vessels of the Jewish Temple and brought them to the house of his god. So did King Antiochus (1 Macc 1:21-23). Daniel tells of a Babylonian king who made an image and demanded that all worship it under penalty of death. So did King Antiochus (1 Macc 1:41-50). Daniel tells of a Babylonian king who plunged from the height of his pride and became mad. So did King Antiochus, whose contemporaries

20. John R. Bartlett, *The First and Second Books of the Maccabees,* p. 10.

actually called him "Epimanes," or "madman" (Polybius *The Histories* 26.10; Athenaeus *Deipnosophistai* 2.45c; 5.193a). Daniel tells of a Babylonian king who committed sacrilege with the Temple vessels and of his swift doom. So did King Antiochus (Josephus, *Antiquities* 12.9.1; Granius Licinianus *Liber* 28). Daniel tells of a Babylonian king who cast Jews into a fiery furnace and into a lion's den and of the ultimate victory of these Jews who survived the threats of fire and beasts. So King Antiochus also cast Jews into similar circumstances of suffering. However, they, too, will come out of the place of suffering into which the wicked king cast them just as victoriously as did Daniel and the Jews of his day.

The lessons which are implicit in the historical events of the sixth-century B.C. Babylonian era concerning the victory of Daniel and his friends and the humiliation of Nebuchadnezzar were made explicit in the defeat of Antiochus IV Epiphanes and the triumph of the people of Judea over Hellenism. Therefore, the cast of characters and events in Daniel previewed the events of the Maccabean era and guaranteed the ultimate victory of the people of God. But to concede a Maccabean application of much of the material in the book of Daniel does not necessarily demand a contemporary authorship of the book. The material in the book, while related to the era of the Antiochus crisis, was written in the sixth century B.C. by the prophet Daniel under the inspiration of the Holy Spirit, and not in the second century B.C. by a pseudonymous Daniel.

Much that they found in the apocalypse of Daniel sustained the Jews during the Antiochus crisis. In like manner, the apocalypse of Daniel, and especially the great New Testament Apocalypse—the book of Revelation—will sustain the Jews during the Antichrist crisis of the end days. While the book of Daniel has much to say about the last days also, it is the book of the Revelation which depicts the events of the Tribulation period (chaps. 6-18), the advent of the Messiah (chap. 19), and the establishment of the Messianic Kingdom on earth (chap. 20).

Having established the relevancy of the book of Daniel to the Maccabean period of Jewish history, we now suggest its relationship to another Old Testament scroll, the book of Esther. These two books apparently united in the Antiochus crisis to provide hope and comfort to the persecuted Jews.

Written against the background of the Persian threat to annihilate the Jews, the mystical message of Esther is that the same God, though His name is never mentioned, who delivered the Jews from the Persians also will deliver the Jews from the threat of the Greeks.

Purim is the Jewish festival which commemorates the deliverance of the Jews from this Persian threat of annihilation. In 161 B.C., three years after the death of King Antiochus IV Epiphanes, we find the first historical record of the observance of Purim (2 Macc 15:36). Perhaps it had been neglected since the days of Esther. But then, the Jews felt a real impetus toward reinstating Purim because they had only recently been delivered from the fulminations of King Antiochus, just as the Jews of Esther's day were delivered from the threats of Haman. This is further evidence indicating how influential the scroll of Esther must have been upon the Jews who were suffering under the evil decrees of Antiochus.

Hanukkah, which commemorates the deliverance of the Temple from Antiochus's defilement, joins Purim as the two great non-Torah feasts which the Jews observe to this day. Purim celebrates the victory of the Jews over the Persians, who tried to destroy their bodies, while Hanukkah celebrates the victory of the Jews over the Greeks, who tried to destroy their souls.

7

The Gezerot: Antiochus's Evil Decrees

And forces shall stand on his part, and they shall profane
the sanctuary, even the fortress, and shall take away the
continual burnt-offering, and they shall set up the abomination that maketh desolate. And such as do wickedly
against the covenant shall he pervert by flatteries (Dan
11:31-32a).

Fulfilled: 168-165 B.C.

IN THE YEAR 168 B.C. Antiochus IV Epiphanes issued his "Evil
Decrees." "Throughout his empire: his subjects were all to
become one people and abandon their own laws and religion"
(1 Macc 1:41).

The consequences which these evil decrees produced among
the Jews lasted for exactly three and one half years. The duration of their suffering ran from Tammuz (June 168 B.C.), until
Heshvan (Oct. 165 B.C.).[1] This will also be the duration of
the Great Tribulation of the end days. This is one of the most
interesting parallels between the two eras. While Antiochus
IV Epiphanes reigned for over eleven years, the length of the
coersive period of his hellenizing pogroms against the Jews
were much less, concentrated into three and one half years.
Jesus indicated that the suffering of the Great Tribulation
will be shortened (Matt 24:22) to the same three-and-one-
half-year period, though the Antichrist will reign during the
entire seventieth week of Daniel (Dan 9:24-27), a period of
seven full years.

1. H. Graetz, *A Popular History of the Jews*, 1:365.

Josephus, to whom we are indebted for his histories, was a Jewish defector to the Romans during the Great Revolt. When the Jews refused to surrender Jerusalem to Titus in A.D. 70, the Roman general set Josephus before the walls of the city in an attempt to persuade his fellow countrymen that to continue resistance was futile. In order to document his case, Josephus resorted to numerous historical illustrations. Among them he made reference to the Antiochus crisis and its duration.

> When Antiochus, who was called Epiphanes, lay before this city, and had been guilty of many indignities against God, and our forefathers met him in arms, they then were slain in the battle, this city was plundered by our enemies, and our sanctuary made desolate for three years and six months.[2]

Graetz confirms Josephus's estimate, saying, "Nearly three and a half years . . . have passed since the persecution began and the Temple was defiled."[3] Speaking of the duration of Antiochus's persecution of the Jews, Professor Bevan also says, "The prediction of Daniel that the tribulation would last three years and a half was thus singularly verified."[4] Of course, Bevan's view of Daniel is typical of the scholarly critic. He sees all of Daniel's "predictions" as having been written by some contemporary after the event had taken place. Nevertheless, as far as the duration of Antiochus's pogrom against the Jews is concerned, Bevan confirms that it lasted for three and one half years.

HELLENIZATION BY FORCE

At that time there appeared in Israel a group of renegade Jews, who incited the people. 'Let us enter into a covenant with the Gentiles round about,' they said, 'because disaster upon disaster has overtaken us since we segre-

2. Josephus *Wars* 5.9.4.
3. Graetz, 1:365.
4. Edwyn R. Bevan, "Syria and the Jews," in *The Cambridge Ancient History,* 8:516.

gated ourselves from them.' The people thought this is a good argument, and some of them in their enthusiasm went to the king and received authority to introduce non-Jewish laws and customs. They built a sports-stadium in the gentile style in Jerusalem. They removed their marks of circumcision and repudiated the holy covenant. They intermarried with Gentiles, and abandoned themselves to evil ways (1 Macc 1:11-15).

This text from the Apocrypha reminds us that Hellenism was not initially forced upon the Jews by the Seleucid tyrant. In fact, the initiative came from within, for it was the Jews themselves who, in about 175 B.C., petitioned Antiochus IV Epiphanes that Jerusalem be granted the status of a Greek polis and that the essential mark of a Hellenistic city, the gymnasium, be constructed there. Though many Jews remained faithful to the covenant and resented their fellow Jews' attempts to introduce Hellenism into Jerusalem, the pro-Greek party, led by Hellenistic high priests Jason and Menelaus, succeeded in implementing the Greek way of life in the Jewish capital between 175 and 170 B.C. But then, in 168 B.C., what some of the Jews themselves introduced and allowed to flourish in Jerusalem was to be used by King Antiochus in an attempt to unify his empire after the disastrous confrontation with the Romans in Egypt on the Day of Eleusis (cf. 2 Macc 4:7-9).

After his rebuff in Egypt, Antiochus realized that the best bulwark against future threats to his empire was to unify his people against the Romans. Judea especially, because it was situated in the gateway to Egypt, had to be solidly Seleucid in its allegiance and uniform in its adherence to the Greek way of life which characterized the rest of the Seleucid Empire. Though many aristocratic Jews had already become Hellenists, the masses of Jewish people were still strong enough to resist the total impact of this victorious Greek culture. These Jews who had maintained their traditional loyalties and orthodox posture in religion also had to bow to the common need—if not willingly, then by force.

The principal strength of these Jews in warding off the effects of Hellenism was their religion. At the same time, Antiochus realized that it was the religious element in Hellenism which had real potential for unifying his empire. A common religion afforded an intangible bond which could weld together his geographically staggering and racially heterogeneous domains.

Only in Judea was this syncretism resisted.

Beginning soon after the Day of Eleusis and continuing for the next three and one half years, Antiochus attempted to force this uniformity of religion upon the Jews. He did not demand that they renounce their God so much as that they renounce the uniqueness of their God and those special observances which emphasized this uniqueness. They were to assimilate Yahweh into the Greek Pantheon. There they could still worship Him, but at the same time they had to recognize the existence of other gods and include them in their worship. In addition, they were to confess the supremacy of Zeus, of whom Antiochus conceived himself to be the incarnate representative on earth.

Most pagan gods—the gods of the captured nations—were easily assimilated into the Greek Pantheon. In many cases local gods were identified with some Greek god, the only difference being in their respective names. However, the Greek religion itself was too unorganized to be an organizational force. A superficial identity between local gods and the Greek gods was not sufficient in itself to unify the people. But the idea of a god-king gave a fixed object of worship among the local cults. Therefore, Antiochus's claim to be God locked in place the unifying power of Hellenistic religion, for it objectified a common allegiance to the throne and gave to this allegiance a religious dynamic with which everyone could identify. All of Antiochus's subjects seemed to have accepted him as God with little conflict. Their gods were not jealous gods, as was Yahweh, the God of Israel, and they passively accommodated this new deity with no traumas. Even the Samaritans addressed Antiochus as "God Manifest."[5]

Southeast of the Acropolis in Athens stood the temple of Zeus Olympius, begun by Pisistratus some 360 years before the time of Antiochus, but as yet unfinished. Antiochus instructed the Roman architect Decimus Cossutius to construct a gigantic temple on the spot. Cossutius designed a beautiful building, surrounded by double columns, not of limestone but of Pentelic marble. A few of these columns stand today in bare isolation. Livy says that the temple was "the only one in the world, the plan of which was suitable to the greatness of the deity."[6] The temple itself was not completed in Antiochus's lifetime. In fact, another 300 years were to pass before Hadrian completed it in A.D. 130. Nevertheless, this endeavor by King Antiochus attracted the attention of the ancient historians more than any of the other enterprises which he undertook.[7] The decision of Antiochus to build this temple in Athens gives evidence that, of all the Greek gods, it was Zeus Olympius for which the king had the most enthusiasm. In addition, Zeus then reappeared upon Seleucid coins where the god had ceased to figure since the days of Seleucus I Nicator, more than a century before. Furthermore, Antiochus was the first Helle-

5. Josephus *Antiquities* 12.5.5.
6. Livy *The History of Rome* 41.20.
7. Polybius *Histories* 26.1.11; Livy, 41.20; Strabo *Geography* 9.1.17; Velleius Paterculus *Historiae Romanae* 1.10.1; Pausanius *Guide to Greece* 1.18.6. Antiochus IV Epiphanes did many other things for Athens, such as presenting the city with a golden aegis with a head of Medusa, which was placed in the south wall of the Acropolis, looking down on the contributed toward the restoration of the Parthenon. (See *American Journal of Archaeology* [1934] pp. 105 ff.) So impressed were the Athenians by his generosity toward them that they issued a decree four years after his death, c. 160 B.C., expressing their gratitude to his daughter on the occasion of her marriage, for all that her father had done for them. But his plans for the temple of Olympian Zeus remained the most impressive.

nistic king to introduce divine epitaphs such as "God Manifest" on his coins.[8]

It is rather apparent that Antiochus thought of himself not as merely a god, but as the earthly manifestation of the supreme god of the Greek Pantheon, Zeus Olympius. This idea was first introduced by Professor Bevan in 1900 and is now the generally accepted interpretation of Antiochus's fantasy.[9]

Of further significance is the fact that Antiochus's claim to be God coincided with his persecution of the Jews. Up until 169 B.C. he was known simply as King Antiochus. However, around this time he added the title "Theos Epiphanes," which means "God Manifest," to his name. This gives rise to the real issue in the Hellenism process. Whom were the Jews to recognize as supreme God: Yahweh, the monotheistic spirit God of Israel; or Zeus Olympius, the pagan god of the Greeks, manifest in the person of King Antiochus?

Many Jews in Jerusalem had already yielded to the Greek Pantheon and were worshiping gods other than Yahweh. They had also given up the distinctive marks of the covenant religion, such as Torah reading, abstinence from certain unclean foods, circumcision, and the Sabbath observance. Many other Jews were to do the same during the next three and one half years under the duress of King Antiochus.

This is also an indication of how events will be during the end days. The Antichrist will turn upon the Jews and severely persecute them during the three and one half years of the Great Tribulation. And his persecution of the Jews will also coincide with his claim to be God. The first division of the seven-year period of the end-time events will feature the Antichrist as a world dictator who will seem altruistic in his attempts to bring about world stability. He will tolerate an apostate world church and a resurgent Jewish orthodoxy as

8. Otto Markholm, *Antiochus IV of Syria,* in Classical Et Mediaevalia, pp. 68 ff.
9. Bevan, 1:155; see also Bevan's "A Note on Antiochus Epiphanes," *The Journal of Hellenic Studies* 20 (1900): 26-28.

allies in this endeavor. He will even allow the rebuilding of the Jewish Temple in Jerusalem and the reinstitution of the Levitical system of sacrifices and offerings. The only religious group which he will persecute during the first half of the seventieth week will be the saints of God, those Jews and Gentiles who accept Jesus as Saviour during those days (Matt 24:9-14).

However, at mid-period his stratagems will change. Then he will claim to be God.

He will destroy the world church and set his image in the Jewish Temple. The sacrifices will cease, just as they did during the Antiochus crisis, and the severe persecution of those Jews who will not accept him as God will begin. These pogroms will last for three and one half years, during which time the Antichrist will attempt to coerce the Jews into accepting an alien religion, the cult of the beast.

The enforced Hellenization of the Jews in the second century B.C. was placed under the direction of two representatives of Antiochus in Jerusalem.

First, King Antiochus located a strong military garrison in the city under the command of General Apollonius. As a token of what was to come, Apollonius ordered a dress parade on the first Sabbath after his arrival. All the Jews who turned out to see it were killed, and the city lay open before him. Syrian troops occupied the city and established headquarters in the Acra (2 Macc 5:24-26).

Second, the destruction of Orthodox Judaism and its replacement by a hellenized Judaism were finally entrusted to one of the king's old friends from Athens. Previously Antiochus had given this responsibility to Philip, a Phrygian who was "by disposition more barbarous than his master" (2 Macc 5:22), and to Andronicus, who was in charge of hellenizing the Samaritans (2 Macc 5:23). However, they were not efficient enough, and "shortly afterwards King Antiochus sent an elderly Athenian to force the Jews to abandon their ancestral customs and no longer regulate their lives according to the laws of God. He was also commissioned to pollute the temple at Jerusalem and dedicate it to Olympian Zeus" (2 Macc 6:1-2). It was the responsibility of this elderly Athenian to enforce the evil decrees of Antiochus which prohibited the Jews from following the traditions of their fathers.

These two aggressions of Antiochus against the Jews were predicted by the prophet Daniel. "They shall profane the sanctuary" (Dan 11:31a) a reference to the elderly Athenian who directed the assault upon Judaism. Second, there was the profaning "even [of] the fortress" (Dan 11:31b) by the garrison of Mysian mercenaries under the command of General Apollonius.

The profaning of the sanctuary and fortress are spoken of in close proximity because the fortress was located on Temple Mount. The whole area was fortified and billeted with soldiers.

> The city of David was turned into a citadel, enclosed by a high stout wall with strong towers, and garrisoned by impious foreigners and renegades. Having made themselves secure, they accumulated arms and provisions, and deposited there the massed plunder of Jerusalem. There they lay in ambush, a lurking threat to the temple and a perpetual menace to Israel (1 Macc 1:33-36).

Apollonius and the elderly Athenian—we know not his name[10]—were charged with the task of hellenizing the Jews by force. They were to see to it that the evil decrees of Antiochus were carried out. The Athenian, an expert in all the tenets of Greek culture, was to apply these principles of Hellenism to the Jewish situation. Apollonius, with the strength of his Mysian garrison, was to see to it that these principles were enforced. Menelaus was also a part of this team, for it was apparently he who identified those Jews who were reluctant to cooperate (2 Macc 6:23). It is these godless Jews, such

10. John R. Bartlett, *The First and Second Books of the Maccabees*, p. 263.

as Menelaus, who are identified by Daniel as "such as do wickedly against the covenant" whom king Antiochus "shall ... pervert by flatteries" (Dan 11:32*a*). Here is the essence of Antichristianism, the coersive attempt to force an alien religion upon the Jewish people. Beginning with the days of Antiochus IV Epiphanes, who attempted to force Hellenism upon the Jews, through the Middle Ages when kings and popes enforced Romanism upon them, until the end time when the false prophet will attempt to impose the cult of the beast upon them, the Jews will contend with these subtle and coersive forces designed to compel them away from the covenant.

One of Israel's most important contributions to civilization has been the house of worship. The Temple was a prototype of both the mosque and the church. When Antiochus desecrated the Temple, he struck at the very heart of the Jews' religion. "This national catastrophe was felt by every Jew within the Hellenistic world," says Moshe Pearlman. "For by now, the second century b.c., the Temple had become more than a central shrine of the Jewish community. It was also the symbolic center of the nation, the focus of their existence as a people."[11]

The Antichrist will do the same, for in the end days he will focus his aggressions upon the Temple where his image will be placed.

ANTIOCHUS'S EVIL DECREES

The king then issued a decree throughout his empire: his subjects were all to become one people and abandon their own laws and religion. The nations everywhere complied with the royal command, and many in Israel accepted the foreign worship, sacrificing to idols and profaning the sabbath. Moreover, the king sent agents with written orders to Jerusalem and the towns of Judaea. Ways and customs foreign to the country were to be in-

11. Moshe Pearlman, *The Maccabees*, p. 65.

troduced. Burnt-offerings, sacrifices, and libations in the temple were forbidden; sabbaths and feast-days were to be profaned; the temple and its ministers to be defiled. Altars, idols, and sacred precincts were to be established; swine and other unclean beasts to be offered in sacrifice. They must leave their sons uncircumcised; they must make themselves in every way abominable, unclean, and profane, and so forget the law and change all their statutes. The penalty for disobedience was death. (1 Macc 1:41-50).

What caused Antiochus IV Epiphanes, who was brought up in the Graeco-Roman tradition of religious toleration, to attack the Law of Moses and to attempt to impose Hellenism upon the Jews as if their religion were criminal or subversive?

Antiochus was as much an enigma to his contemporaries as he is today. Some would blame his evil decrees upon his degenerate character, and especially on the traumatic effect which the Day of Eleusis had upon him. Since he could not vent himself upon the Romans, he took out his spite upon the Jews. Again, some charge him with excessive devotion to Hellenism. As the ancient world's hellenizer par excellence,[12] he realized that Greek culture would never conquer the Jews. Over a century and a half had passed since Alexander the Great had introduced Hellenism into the Near East, and it still had not fully inundated Judaism. So King Antiochus, the ardent philhellenic, probably felt he had to force the issue if he were to realize his goal of a completely hellenized empire.[13]

But, in reality, his purpose was more practical than ideal. He had to unify his empire against future threats by Rome, and the best way to do it was by hellenizing it.[14] His evil

12. Polybius *Histories* 29.9.13; Livy, 41.20.
13. Bevan, "Syria and the Jews," in *The Cambridge Ancient History*, 8:499; William Tarn and G. T. Griffith, *Hellenistic Civilization*, pp. 215, 338; Solomon Zeitlin, *The Rise and Fall of the Judean State*, 1:77; J. W. Swain, "Antiochus Epiphanes and Egypt," *Classical Philology*, 39 (1944): 73-94.
14. W. O. E. Oesterley and T. H. Robinson, A History of Israel, 2:222; W. W. Tarn, *The Greeks in Bactria and India*, p. 186.

decrees were designed to rid his empire of its most outstanding threat to unity and its most intransigent resistance to the Greek way: Judaism. Just as a century or so later, the resistance of the Jews contributed significantly to the loss of prestige and, finally, to the decline and fall of the Roman Empire,[15] so the resistance of the Jews was a constant threat to the stability of Antiochus's empire.

The Apocrypha indicates that Antiochus's evil decrees had several aspects. These features also will figure prominently in the pogroms of the Antichrist, for he, too, will resort to some of the same coercive measures as did Antiochus.

First, there was the destruction of the Torah scrolls. "All scrolls of the law which were found were torn up and burnt. Anyone discovered in possession of a Book of the Covenant, or conforming to the law, was put to death" (1 Macc 1:55-57). Later, during the Roman period, the desecration of the Torah scrolls became the dramatic witness to the submission of the Jews.[16] In the Temple the Torah scrolls were first defiled with the grease from pigs offered upon the sacred altar, and then they were burned to indicate Antiochus's contempt for the Law. "For the first time the Torah was baptized in fire," observes Graetz.[17] As a commentary on the advance of civilization, the Nazis did the same thing over 2,000 years later. However, the Jews made some recovery from this first blow—the loss of the Torah—in an ingenius way. They invented the haftarah. By the time of Jesus it was customary in Jewish synagogues to read from the prophets as well as from the Torah (Luke 4:16-19). These readings from the prophets are called haftarah. In the Middle Ages the rabbis said that these haftarah readings from the prophets originated during the Antiochus crisis when he forbade the Torah to be read.[18] By reading those passages in the prophets which either reflect,

15. Max I. Dimont, *Jews, God and History,* p. 149.
16. Josephus *Antiquities* 20.5.4; *Wars* 2.12.2; 8.5.5; *Gittin* 56b.
17. Graetz, 1:346.
18. J. H. Hertz, *The Pentateuch and Haftorahs,* p. 20.

quote, or paraphrase passages from the Pentateuch, the Jews could retain the Torah reading in this veiled form. The haftarah is still read in traditional synagogues today. Second, Antiochus's decrees enforced the eating of swine's flesh.

> And so the tyrant Antiochus, sitting with his counsellors upon a lofty place and surrounded by his soldiers under arms, ordered his guards to hale the Hebrews one by one, and force them to eat of swine's flesh and of meat consecrated to idols; and those who refused to eat of the contamination he ordered to be broken on the wheel and killed (4 Macc 5:1-3; cf. 1 Macc 1:62).

Eleazar, a priest and leading teacher of the Law, was martyred in the presence of Antiochus IV Epiphanes (2 Macc 6:18-30; 4 Macc 5:1—7:23). He was in his ninetieth year when he was ordered to eat swine's flesh. Refusing, he was sent to the rack, where he died willingly rather than obey the evil decrees of Antiochus.

Enraged because of Eleazar's defiance, Antiochus ordered other Hebrews to be similarly tested. Seven brothers were brought before him and challenged to eat pork. They refused. The seven, along with their mother, were martyred (2 Macc 7:1-42; 4 Macc 8:1—18:24; cf. Josephus *Wars* 2.8.10).

Some months later, in 164 B.C. when the Maccabean revolt proved to be a real threat to Antiochus's control of Judea, the king wrote a letter to the Jewish people in which he offered to relax this part of his evil decrees (2 Macc 11:27-33). His purpose was to weaken Jewish resistance by encouraging the people to return home. Therefore he offered to repeal the prohibition on Jewish food laws. It did not work, for the offer came too late.

Third, "They must leave their sons uncircumcised," said the decree (1 Macc 1:48). Many hellenized Jews had already "removed their marks of circumcision" (1:15). But now, this unique mark of the covenant was forbidden. "In accordance with the royal decree, they put to death women who had had their children circumcised. Their babies, their families, and those who had circumcised them, they hanged by the neck" (1:60-61). On one occasion two women who had circumcised their infants were caught. They were paraded through the streets of Jerusalem with their babies tied to their breasts and then led to the pinnacle of the Temple and from there cast down into the Kedron Valley (2 Macc 6:10).

Fourth, "It was forbidden either to observe the sabbath or to keep the traditional festivals" (2 Macc 6:6; 1 Macc 1:43). On numerous occasions Jews who were caught observing the Sabbath were mercilessly punished. A large group of Jews, for example, was found in a cave, observing this holy day. When ordered to come out, they refused either to come out or to defend themselves. Antiochus's soldiers set fire to the cave's entrance, thus suffocating more than a thousand people (1 Macc 2:29-38; 2 Macc 5:11). As a result of this massacre, Mattathias and his followers decided that they must defend themselves on the Sabbath or the Jewish people would be completely annihilated (1 Macc 2:39-41).

This massacre was an important factor in the Maccabean revolt. Rebellion had been seething for some time. However, the Jews faced two problems. First, they had no leader. The events in Modin were soon to provide one, for Judas Maccabee, Israel's greatest warrior, would be thrust forth to lead the Jewish rebellion. The other problem was the sanctity of the Sabbath. Heretofore the Jews had refused to defend themselves on the Sabbath, making a successful insurrection impossible. However, soon after the revolt started in Modin, old Mattathias, a priest, issued a statement encouraging the Jews to take up arms if they were attacked on the Sabbath.

Apparently the observance of the Sabbath will emerge once again to complicate the escape of the Jews during the Great Tribulation. Jesus said, "And pray ye that your flight be not in the winter, neither on a sabbath" (Matt 24:20). This indicates that the question of self-preservation on the Sabbath may once more impede the Jews who will be under the tyranny of the Antichrist. This could jeopardize the survival of Orthodox Jews just as it did during the Antiochus crisis of the second century B.C.

The Jews not only were forbidden to observe the Sabbath and their other holy days, but they also were forced to participate in pagan festivals. Once a month the birthday of King Antiochus was celebrated. The Jews, on that day, were driven by brute force to eat the entrails of the sacrificial victims. When the pagan feast of Dionysus was observed, the Jews were forced to join in the procession and to wear ivy wreaths in honor of the pagan god (2 Macc 6:7). This not only went on in Jerusalem, but our sources indicate that the Jewish inhabitants of all the Greek cities were forced to participate in these pagan practices (6:8-9).

Fifth, the king made the morning and evening sacrifices to cease. "Burnt-offerings, sacrifices, and libations in the temple were forbidden" (1 Macc 1:45) by the evil decrees of Antiochus. These sacrifices had continued uninterrupted for several centuries, beginning with the returning exiles. The first caravan of Jews who returned from Babylon in 538 B.C., upon entering the land, agreed to reinstitute the services of worship. When they gathered that autumn at the Temple site in Jerusalem, the debris was cleared away from the middle of the ruined courts, and a rough altar was established. From that time forward, for a period of 350 years, the regular sequence of sacrifices, morning and evening, went on uninterrupted until the evil decrees of King Antiochus terminated them.

However, about the time the continual burnt offerings were begun after the Exile, Daniel was receiving this revelation from God about their future termination. He predicted that the Seleucid tyrant would "take away the continual burnt-offering" (11:31). This prophecy was literally fulfilled in

168 B.C., three and one half centuries after Daniel predicted it. However, the worst indignity of all was that portion of the evil decrees which ordered the desecration of the Temple. The elderly Athenian was "commissioned to pollute the temple at Jerusalem and dedicate it to Olympian Zeus" (2 Macc 6:2). Daniel also saw this desecration of the sacred sanctuary and predicted that "they . . . shall take away the continual burnt-offering, and they shall set up the abomination that maketh desolate" (Dan 11:31*b*).

The pollution of the Temple was designed to eliminate the Jews' rallying point. It took several forms.

The Gentiles were given free access to the Temple. Previously only the covenant people could enter into any portion of the Temple, while only the priests could penetrate within the veil to the Holy of Holies. But now Gentiles were permitted to turn the Temple into a place of licentious revelry. Sacred prostitution operated freely in its hallowed precincts. Not since before the Exile had ritual prostitution been practiced in Israel, and then only in pagan groves. In those days it was denounced by the prophet Hosea (Hos 4:11-14). But now sacred prostitution flourished in the Temple which had been transformed into a Gentile house of pagan worship (2 Macc 6:3-4).

"They also brought forbidden things inside, and heaped the altar with impure offerings prohibited by the law" (6:5). These impure offerings were composed of swine and other unclean beasts (1 Macc 1:47). Nothing could have been more abhorrent to the Jews than the body of a pig offered in sacrifice to a pagan god upon the sacred altar of the Temple of the Lord. Its blood was sprinkled on the altar. Its meat was cooked and the broth poured upon the Torah scrolls.[19] Menelaus and the other hellenized priests partook of the swine meat. No previous desecration could match this one. It

19. Graetz, 1:346.

seemed that King Antiochus could do no more to heap further indignities upon the Jews.

However, an event so devastating to the Jews then took place that even the day on which it occurred is remembered in our sources. "On the fifteenth day of the month Kislev in the year 145, the abomination of desolation was set up on the altar" (1 Macc 1:54). A number of months after the evil decrees were issued—the date was December 7, 168 b.c.—Daniel's prophecy came to pass. In the year 539 b.c. Daniel envisioned the abomination of desolation desecrating the Temple. And, 372 years later, his prophecy was literally fulfilled, for he predicted that "they shall set up the abomination that maketh desolate" (Dan 11:31*b*).

What was it?

Farmer says, "Daniel's 'abomination that maketh desolate' was quite likely, from the Hellenistic point of view, some perfectly rational, good and just modification in the equipment and/or the ritual of the Jerusalem sanctuary. But to the pious Torah-loving Jew it was the acme of blasphemy."[20] Since we cannot be sure just what the abomination was, we might speculate that it was some sort of image which represented both Zeus Olympius and Antiochus. The same sort of representation appears on the coins of this era for they bear the image of a Zeus who has many of Antiochus's features. The establishment of the abomination of desolation in the Temple not only enshrined King Antiochus as the god Zeus, but it also tended to identify Yahweh, the God of the Jews, with Zeus, the god of the Greeks. Roth describes the abomination as

> a bearded image of this pagan deity (Zeus), perhaps in the likeness of Antiochus himself, set up on the altar and the Jews were informed that this was the god of heaven whom they were henceforth to revere. Amongst themselves, they referred to it with a shudder of horror as the Abomination of Desolation.[21]

20. William H. Farmer, *Maccabees, Zealots and Josephus*, p. 86.
21. Cecil Roth, *A Short History of the Jewish People*, p. 69.

In his prophecy Daniel indicated that the abomination would be the ultimate blasphemous act of the coming Gentile ruler, Antiochus IV Epiphanes. Jesus picked up this prophecy of Daniel's, which was fulfilled in the Antiochus crisis of the second century B.C., and reissued it relative to the Antichrist crisis of the end days. In fact, Jesus indicated that the establishment of this new abomination is to signal the beginning of the Great Tribulation period.

> When therefore ye see the abomination of desolation, which was spoken of through Daniel the prophet, standing in the holy place . . . then shall be great tribulation, such as hath not been from the beginning of the world until now, no, nor ever shall be (Matt 24:15, 21).

The abomination of desolation epitomizes the suffering of the Jews during the era of Antiochus. Jesus said that a similar phenomenon is to recur in Jewish history, and, therefore, an abomination of desolation will also epitomize the Great Tribulation of Jewish suffering in the last days.

RELIGIOUS MARTYRDOM BEGINS

The evil decrees of Antiochus IV Epiphanes meant that the Jews were the first people in history to suffer persecution for purely religious reasons, and Antiochus was the first ruler in history to force a religion, under threat of death, upon a subject people.[22]

> Judaism thus witnessed the origin of heroic martyrdom, which was to become a distinguishing feature of the later epochs of its history. The Jews set an example to the world of how not only individual, but whole masses, could consciously suffer for a lofty ideal; how they could relinquish all earthly blessings, endure torture, and die, rather than betray what they regarded as true and sacred. It was better to forfeit one's life than the meaning of life: this was the motto

22. Edwyn R. Bevan, *Jerusalem Under the High Priests,* p. 83; Zeitlin, 1:92; Pearlman, p. 48.

which from then on urged thousands of faithful believers towards the gallows, the guillotine, the *autos-da-fe* in the name of religious, national, and political ideals. The Jewish martyrology has its beginning in the time of Antiochus Epiphanes.[23]

Once again the prefiguring nature of the Antiochus crisis is seen as it reflects the religious persecutions which will take place in the end days. Where religious martyrdom began in the Antiochus crisis of 168-165 B.C., it will end in the Great Tribulation. The *first* people to be persecuted for purely religious reasons were the Jews. They will also be the *last* people to be persecuted for religious reasons. During the Great Tribulation period the Antichrist will dissolve all other religions and will demand that he alone be worshiped as God. Those Jews who do not conform will be killed (Rev 13:15).

This unprecedented persecution of the Jews for exclusively religious reasons seems to have been an enforced policy all over Antiochus's empire and not just in Judea.[24] This would account for the persistent tradition that the martyrdom of Eleazar and the seven brothers did not occur in Judea, but in Antioch. The tombs of these martyrs are still shown in that city, located in the synagogue Kenesheth Hashmunith, which was named for the mother of the Maccabees. Malalas also records this tradition.[25]

The persecution of the Jews during the end time by the Antichrist will also be universal. However, its most intense manifestation will be in Israel, and particularly in Jerusalem.

The nations—expressly the Idumaeans, the Ammonites, the Philistines, and the Phoenicians—gave no solace to the Jews who fled the wrath of King Antiochus during those days of

23. Simon Dobnov, *History of the Jews*, 1:488.
24. Matthew Spinka and Glanville Downey, trans., *Chronicle of John Malalas, Books VIII-XVIII*, p. 111n.
25. Malalas *Chronicle of John Malalas* 206:20-22; 207:10-13; see J. Obermann, "The Sepulchre of the Maccabean Martyrs," *The Journal of Biblical Literature*, 51 (1932): 250-65. But cf. 4 Macc 18:5, which infers that the martyrdom occurred in Jerusalem.

persecution. Rather, egged on by Lysias, Antiochus's field commander in Judea at that time, these Gentile nations terrorized the fleeing Jews. They raided Jewish territory and victimized the Jews whom they caught there. They gave asylum to the Greek troops and to Hellenistic traitors. This caused Judas Maccabee to retaliate later on. He sacked Idumaean strongholds, defeated a large number of Ammonites, drove the Philistines back to the coast, and, to punish them, he destroyed the city of Ashdod and burned the Philistine fleet in the harbor of Jaffa.

In the end days the reaction of the Jews to the persecutions of the Antichrist will be traditional and therefore predictable. There is a response which seems to have been preconditioned in the Jews, namely, to flee to the desert when the Temple is in danger. It may reflect an innate belief that, though God has abandoned the Temple, He can be found again where Israel first tabernacled with Him—in the wilderness (cf. Deut 32:7-14). When Titus burned the Temple, the people implored him that they might be allowed to flee into the wilderness.[26] Excavations in the wilderness of Judea, carried on by Professor Yadin of Hebrew University, have uncovered many artifacts from the Bar Kochba era. The caves of that region were occupied by refugees from Judea and Jerusalem who fled the Romans during the Bar Kochba revolt and after the fall of Betar in A.D. 135.[27]

They did the same thing in the time of Antiochus IV Epiphanes. "At that time many who wanted to maintain their religion and law went down to the wilds to live there" (1 Macc 2:29).

Consistent with this predilection of the Jews, we find that Jesus instructed the Great Tribulation inhabitants of Jeru-

26. Josephus *Wars* 7.6.3.
27. Josephus records the recurrence of this tendency to flee into the wilderness in time of persecution in *Antiquities* 20.5.1; 20.8.6; 20.8.10; and *Wars* 12:13.4; 6.6.3.

salem also to flee from the Antichrist into the wilderness, just as the Jews did during the Antiochus crisis. Jesus said,

> When therefore ye see the abomination of desolation, which was spoken of through Daniel the prophet, standing in the holy place (let him that readeth understand), then let them that are in Judea flee unto the mountains: let him that is on the housetop not go down to take out things that are in his house: and let him that is in the field not return back to take his cloak. But woe unto them that are with child and to them that give suck in those days! And pray ye that your flight be not in the winter, neither on a sabbath: for then shall be great tribulation (Matt 24:15-21).

This age-old inclination of the Jews to flee Jerusalem and Judea when the Temple is desecrated has a corresponding implication concerning the Gentiles and their responsibility to the Jews in such an hour. If the tendency to flee when the Temple is in danger prevails among the Jews, then there may be a related obligation which has been providentially laid upon the Gentiles, a sort of Anne Frank syndrome in which the Gentiles are to be held accountable for providing aid and comfort to the fleeing Jew. The prophet Isaiah may have been articulating this principle when he said,

> Give counsel, execute justice; make thy shade as the night in the midst of the noonday; hide the outcasts; betray not the fugitive. Let mine outcasts dwell with thee; as for Moab, be thou a covert to him from the face of the destroyer (Isa 16:3-4).

The prophet was addressing Judah, indicating that she had a responsibility to receive the fleeing Moabites, just as the Moabites will have a duty during the Great Tribulation to receive the Jews who will be fleeing from the face of the destroyer. If the Moabites be extinct, then it will be incumbent upon those who will be occupying their territory, east and south of the Dead Sea, to fulfill this obligation.

Jesus also enunciated this principle of Gentile responsibility, for He indicated that the judgment of the nations will have as its theme the Gentile treatment of the fleeing Jew, particularly during the Great Tribulation (Matt 25:31-46).

The Great Tribulation flight of the Jews is depicted in the book of Revelation under the figure of a woman (Israel) who gives birth to a man-child (the Lord Jesus Christ). After the birth of the child she is driven into the wilderness. Since Israel is in view here, the age of the Church is passed over unseen, and events in Israel move from the first-century birth of Christ to the end days when the Jews will flee into the wilderness for a time, and times, and a half time, that is, for the three and one half years of the Great Tribulation period.

> And when the dragon saw that he was cast down to the earth, he persecuted the woman that brought forth the man child. And there were given to the woman the two wings of a great eagle, that she might fly into the wilderness unto her place, where she is nourished for a time, and times, and half a time, from the face of the serpent. And the serpent cast out of his mouth after the woman water as a river, that he might cause her to be carried away by the stream. And the earth helped the woman, and the earth opened her mouth and swallowed up the river which the dragon cast out of his mouth. And the dragon waxed wroth with the woman, and went away to make war with the rest of her seed, that keep the commandments of God, and hold the testimony of Jesus (Rev 12:13-17).

The evil decrees of Antiochus threatened the Jews with spiritual genocide. If they refused to yield, they faced an option of physical genocide. The same option will obtain for the Jews during the Great Tribulation.

However, the Great Tribulation microcosm in the second century B.C. proved that Jewish survival is possible when they are faced with the option of apostasy or extinction. They will survive also when the same alternatives are imposed upon them by the Antichrist in the end days.

8

Judas Maccabee: Israel's Great Deliverer

But the people that know their God shall be strong, and
do exploits. And they that are wise among the people
shall instruct many; yet they shall fall by the sword and
by flame, by captivity, and by spoil, many days. Now
when they shall fall, they shall be helped with a little
help; but many shall join themselves unto them with flatteries. And some of them that are wise shall fall, to refine
them, and to purify, and to make them white, even to the
time of the end; because it is yet for the time appointed
(Dan 11:32*b*-35).

Fulfilled: 165 B.C.

EACH YEAR on a cold December night in Israel as the stars first
appear, a torch is lit in the little village of Modin, the birth-
place and burial ground of the Maccabees. It is carried by
runner to Ben Gurion International Airport. Extinguished,
this torch is taken aboard an El Al flight to New York. Arriving at Kennedy International, it is handed over to the Masada
Youth Group which relays the rekindled flame to every major
Jewish community in America to aid in the celebration of
Judaism's second most popular festival, Hanukkah.

Hanukkah is derived from a Hebrew word which means
"dedication." An eight-day festival, it is celebrated by the
Jews in memory of the deliverance of their forefathers from
the cruel tyrant Antiochus IV Epiphanes. Hanukkah is also
known as the "Feast of Dedication" and the "Festival of
Lights." It begins on the twenty-fifth day of the Jewish month

Kislev. Since the Jewish calendar is based on the moon rather than the sun, all Jewish holidays fall on different days each year. Hanukkah is usually in December.

The observance of the festival centers around the lighting of the menorah, which holds nine candles. The center candle, the shammash, is used to light the others, one each night until all eight are glowing. At sundown the head of the household lights the first candle as the rest of the family gathers around. An appropriate blessing is said, and then, while the candle burns, the Jewish family enjoys a meal and engages in a game using the dreidel, a Yiddish name for the four-sided top which is spun. On each side of this top appear Hebrew letters which stand for *Nes Gadol Haya Sham,* "A Great Miracle Happened There."

The "Great Miracle" refers to the legend which has persisted among the Jews concerning the cleansing of the Temple. After the Maccabees had recovered the Temple from the Greeks, the time came to reinstitute the Levitical services, but no holy oil could be found for the menorah, the seven-stemmed lampstand. Finally, a cruse of oil, which had been sanctified by the priests and sealed years before, was located. However, the cruse contained just enough oil for one day. But, as if by miracle, the oil continued to burn for eight days. The memory of that miracle is perpetuated today when, in each Jewish home, the Hanukkah candles are lit.

Other traditions also serve to remind the Jews of the great deliverance won by the Maccabees. The meal which is eaten while the candles burn is usually of pancakes called latkes. It is believed that the wives of the Maccabees fed such pancakes to the fighters because it was a meal which could be quickly prepared. The oil used in frying these latkes is also symbolic of the oil which burned for eight days.

Some purely local tradition also has built up around the observance of Hanukkah. There is the Kurdish custom where children burn a doll at the end of the Hanukkah week. This doll is made of wood and rags and is complete with beard, holding a large candle in its hands. The children march through the streets with this doll each night of Hanukkah. At the end of the festival the doll's beard is torn out; it is then set on fire as the children cry, "Antiochus! Antiochus!" This is Hanukkah today.

Twenty-one centuries have passed since the first Hanukkah when the great miracle is said to have happened.

It was late fall in the year 165 B.C. Judas Maccabee and his army of Jewish insurgents approached Jerusalem from the southwest. They had just defeated Antiochus's Greek forces for the fourth time at Beth Zur. Daniel saw them as "the people who know their God [who] shall be strong, and do exploits" (11:32b). There remained yet another Greek force to reckon with behind the formidable Acra fortress within the desolate city.

But, for then, Judas crossed the broken walls of Jerusalem which the Seleucids had destroyed in a previous rage. He headed straight for the sanctuary located across a narrow valley from the menacing Greek fortress. Emerging on Temple Mount, "they found the temple laid waste, the altar profaned, the gates burnt down, the courts overgrown like a thicket or wooded hill-side, and the priests' rooms in ruin" (1 Macc 4:38).

Even while the Jews were on Temple Mount lamenting its desolation, the Greek mercenaries, fortified in the Acra only a short distance southwest of the Temple, rained down arrows upon Judas and his men. This Acra garrison was the last vestige of Greek resistance to Jewish independence left in the land, at least for the time. Josephus says that Judas "chose out some soldiers, and gave them order to fight against those guards that were in the citadel, until he could have purified the temple."[1]

---

1. Josephus *Antiquities* 12.7.6.

THE MACCABEAN REVOLT

Now when they shall fall, they shall be helped with a
little help (Dan 11:34*a*).

Several years prior to this time the Maccabean revolt—the
"little help" of Daniel's vision—had begun in the little village
of Modin.

Not since the time of Nebuchadnezzar, 400 years before,
had the Jews been sufficiently provoked to armed revolt. But,
in 168 B.C., they took up arms against the tyranny of Antiochus
IV Epiphanes. Their next oppressors would be the Romans,
against whom they would also revolt in A.D. 66-70 and again in
A.D. 132-35. From this, the Great Revolt, the Jews were sent
into their second exile which would last for nearly 2,000 years.
Not until the twentieth century would Jews again take up
arms against an oppressor, though they were to be maltreated
during the great exile which stretched between A.D. 70 and
World War II.

First, the Jews took up arms in a token revolt against the
Nazis in World War II.[2] Then, finally, the Jews fought against
Arab oppression on four different occasions: 1948, 1956, 1967,
and 1973 in order to maintain the independence of the State
of Israel. In each instance Gentile tyranny necessitated hostilities. The Jews were never armed aggressors. Though they
may have started the actual conflict—as they did in Modin and
in the case of the Great Revolt and the Six-Day War—the
underlying cause of each clash was Gentile provocation.

The first combat in 168 B.C. was guerrilla warfare in which
the Seleucid occupiers of Judea were harassed by a growing
band of Jewish renegades. Greek patrols were cut down. The
Maccabees also swooped down on isolated villages, destroying
pagan altars and punishing Jewish collaborators. Children,
whose circumcision had been neglected because of the evil
decrees of King Antiochus, were now forcibly circumcised.

2. Leon Uris, *Mila 18*, p. 449.

This revolt began when a band of Seleucid soldiers showed up in the country hamlet of Modin. The villagers were ordered into the town square and Mattathias, a priest with five sons who had recently fled Jerusalem, was singled out for an address by the king's officer.

'You are a leader here,' they [the Greeks in command] said, 'a man of mark and influence in this town, with your sons and brothers at your back. You be the first now to come forward and carry out the king's order. All the nations have done so, as well as the leading men of Judaea and the people left in Jerusalem. Then you and your sons will be enrolled among the King's Friends; you will all receive high honours, rich rewards of silver and gold, and many further benefits.'

To this Mattathias replied in a ringing voice: 'Though all the nations within the king's dominions obey him and forsake their ancestral worship, though they have chosen to submit to his commands, yet I and my sons and brothers will follow the covenant of our fathers. Heaven forbid we should ever abandon the law and its statutes. We will not obey the command of the king, nor will we deviate one step from our forms of worship' (1 Macc 2:17-22) .

The retort of the defiant patriarch created a situation in which the old priest had to be severely rebuked, for others might follow his rebellious example.

However, the tension was suddenly eased when another Jew stepped forward and agreed to make the offering. Inflamed with zeal, Mattathias fell upon this compromising Jew and slew him upon the altar. He also killed the king's commissioner and then pulled down the altar, the hated symbol of Antiochus's oppression.

Then Mattathias cried throughout the city, "Follow me, . . . every one of you who is zealous for the law and strives to maintain the covenant" (1 Macc 2:27). After that he and his sons took to the hills.

The Maccabean revolt had begun.

Their base of operation during the first year of revolution seems to have been the hills of Gophna, which lay just beyond the Judean border in southern Samaria, thirteen miles northeast of Modin. In those days the area was covered with a vast forest.

Mattathias was not to finish the uprising which he had so dramatically begun, for in the 146th year of Greek dominion, he called his sons to his side and said, "But now, my sons, be zealous for the law, and give your lives for the covenant of your fathers. Then Mattathias blessed them, and was gathered to his fathers" (2:50, 69). Mattathias's body was carried by his sons down from the Gophna hills late at night. Moving silently through the deserted streets of Modin, they buried the old rebel priest in the family tomb just outside the village.

"Then Judas [Judah] Maccabaeus came forward in his father's place" (3:1). Judas was named "the hammerer." The Hebrew word for "hammer" is *makabah*. He and his followers are still known as "The Maccabees."

THE BATTLE OF GOPHNA
(1 Macc 3:10-12)

A year or so of harassing the Greek garrison in Jerusalem— though the rebels did not venture to attack the city itself during those days—caused the Seleucid commander in the Jewish capital to send north for reinforcements.

General Apollonius, whose headquarters by that time were in Samaria, responded. The Maccabees were then to face their first frontal engagement with the armies of Antiochus IV Epiphanes. A strong force marched south, taking the direct route between Samaria and Jerusalem which led through the Judean hills.

Judas's army was not as formidable as the forces of King Antiochus. However, he made up for the lack by instilling a sense of zeal in his followers, something which the Greek mercenaries could never duplicate. Judas displayed Torah scrolls which had been desecrated by Antiochus's men who had drawn idols on them. He showed them the Levitical vestments, reminding them that their priests could no longer minister in the Temple. By this means the zeal of his men was stirred. While the Greeks fought for money, defending political principles in which they had little interest, the Jews were fighting a holy war.

On flat ground Antiochus's Macedonian phalanx was awesome. Its might was impregnable as long as it could maneuver in open country. However, Judas decided to surprise General Apollonius in a defile which passed through the Gophna hills. The Greeks were routed. Many were slain, while others escaped and straggled back to Samaria. Apollonius was killed. Judas took the general's sword and used it in battle during the rest of his life.

With the exception of Jerusalem, the rebel Jews were now in firm control of Judea. In Jerusalem, the Greek occupation forces were bottled up, helpless in the Acra. They were unable to venture beyond the broken walls of the city.

In King Antiochus's court there was disconcertion, but not alarm.

THE BATTLE OF BETH-HORON
(1 Macc 3:13-24)

The defeat of Apollonius was considered a minor mishap which could be corrected. The man chosen to put down the Jewish mutiny was General Seron, commander of the Seleucid forces in all the western and southern portion of Antiochus's empire.

Judas and his army met him in the pass of Beth-horon.

A thousand years before, Joshua had put the Amorites to flight in Beth-horon. Here the Jews would also defeat the Twelfth Roman Legion, retreating from an unsuccessful siege of Jerusalem in A.D. 66. At Beth-horon 1,300 years later, Richard the Lion-Hearted would break through the Muslim defenses. Here, General Allenby advanced toward the fall of Jerusalem in World War I. In this famous pass a mechanized infantry, taking the same route which General Seron had taken twenty-one centuries before, routed the Arab defenders of Beth-horon on the night of June 5, 1967, clearing the way for the capture of Jerusalem.

Near Ben Gurion International Airport at Lod, General Seron broke camp and marched toward Beth-horon. Judas's surprise assault was devastating. Again the Greeks were routed, and Seron was killed.

THE BATTLE OF EMMAUS
(1 Macc 3:25–4:27)

The gravity of the rebellion in Judea was finally recognized by the imperial court in Antioch. At this time Antiochus IV Epiphanes was absent from the capital, fighting the Persians in the east. Lysias, whom Antiochus had left to govern his territories west of the Euphrates, raised a large army which was placed under the command of three generals, Ptolemaeus, Nicanor, and Gorgias. They turned south in pursuit of the Jewish rebels. Evading the rugged mountains, whose passes had proved fatal to previous Seleucid forces, the Greek army marched down the coast. East of Jerusalem they camped at Emmaus. The general's strategy was to set up a base camp at the foot of the hills from which they could assault the enemy in the mountains between the coast and Jerusalem. Linking up with the garrison in the Acra, they would then carry out the orders of King Antiochus to systematically exterminate the population of Judea, for, before he left, Antiochus had said, "Break and destroy the strength of Israel and those who are left in Jerusalem, to blot out all memory of them from the place . . . settle foreigners in all their territory, and allot the land to settlers" (1 Macc 3:35-36) .

General Nicanor was so certain of victory this time that he invited slave dealers to accompany his army for an on-the-spot

sale of Jewish captives (2 Macc 8:11). The price of these
Jewish slaves had already been posted in nearby cities.

Hearing that the Maccabees were camped at Mizpeh, General Gorgias took 5,000 foot soldiers and 1,000 horsemen by
night and proceeded toward the rebel encampment, while
General Nicanor's forces remained bivouacked at Emmaus.
However, Judas, having learned of the division of the Greek
forces, attacked the base camp and defeated General Nicanor
who commanded the remaining contingent. Gorgias, finding
Judas's camp at Mizpeh deserted, returned to Emmaus. From
the hilltop he saw his own camp ablaze, with Nicanor and his
soldiers fleeing in disarray. Gorgias and his men joined them
in flight.

For the third time Antiochus's forces had failed to put down
the Maccabean revolt and relieve the beleaguered garrison in
the Acra.

Survivors of the Battle of Emmaus wandered back to Antioch and "reported to Lysias all that had happened" (1 Macc
4:26).

<h3 style="text-align:center">THE BATTLE OF BETH ZUR</h3>
(1 Macc 4:28-35)

"In the following year he gathered sixty thousand picked
infantry and five thousand cavalry to make war on the Jews.
They marched into Idumaea, and encamped at Bethsura,
where Judas met them with ten thousand men" (1 Macc
4:28-29).

Beth Zur lies seventeen miles *southwest* of Jerusalem. This
means that Lysias bypassed the direct route through the hills
of Judea, impressed, no doubt, with the futility of engaging
the rebels in their own territory, the hills north of Jerusalem.
His intention was to approach Jerusalem from the south
where Judas was weakest, liberate the Acra, and then, with
these Greek reinforcements, take out after the insurgent Jews
in the hill country of Judea.

As Lysias's army drew within several miles of Jerusalem, somewhere in the vicinity of Beth Zur, they were sighted by the Maccabees. Judas lifted up his voice in prayer:

> 'All praise to thee, the Saviour of Israel, who didst break the attack of the giant by thy servant David. Thou didst deliver the army of the Philistines into the power of Saul's son, Jonathan, and of his armour-bearer. In like manner put this army into the power of thy people Israel. Humble their pride in their forces and their mounted men. Strike them with panic, turn their insolent strength to water, make them reel under a crushing defeat. Overthrow them by the sword of those who love thee, and let all who know thy name praise thee with songs of thanksgiving' (1 Macc 4:30-33).

An attack by Judas and 10,000 Jewish rebels followed. The Seleucid army was put to flight, with the loss of nearly 5,000 men, according to the Apocrypha (1 Macc 4:34).

Lysias returned to Antioch.

For the first time the Maccabees could relax. Two years would pass before the rebels again would face another Greek force.

From the Battle of Beth Zur, Judas and his men marched up the road to Jerusalem where they prepared to reclaim and cleanse the Temple which Antiochus had defiled three and one half years earlier.

This scene was to be repeated again.

It was nightfall on June 6, 1967. The Jordanian Old City of Jerusalem was surrounded by the army of Israel. From the Mount of Olives, Israeli soldiers looked westward, beyond the Kedron Valley, beyond the walls, toward the Old City, into Temple Mount itself. The night was illuminated by rockets and gunfire. And then came the dawn, the dawn of the greatest day in Israel's history since that day in 165 B.C. when the Maccabees recaptured the Temple area. The military orders of the day started crisply, "We are about to take the Temple

Mount. This is an historic task. The Jewish people are pray-
ing for our victory. All Israel awaits it."

At 8:30 A.M., June 7, 1967 bombardment began, but it was
cut short as Colonel Mordaci Gur, commander of the ground
forces, ordered his tanks across the valley. Leading his troops
in a halftrack, Colonel Gur approached the Lion's Gate which
penetrates the eastern wall of the Old City. It stood ajar. The
halftrack pushed it open and entered the Old City, stopping
before Haramesh-Sherif, the Temple Mount. The holy place
was again in Israeli hands after so many centuries.

Crossing the Haram, Temple Mount, Israeli foot soldiers
streamed down the western side of the plateau to the massive
retaining wall which has shored up Temple Mount ever since
Herod the Great built it in the first century B.C. Those young
Jewish soldiers had heard of it but had never seen it. They
wept as they caressed the sacred stones, intoning prayers of
thanksgiving in Hebrew.

The feelings which flooded Judas and his men were much
the same. However, the sight which greeted them when they
finally recaptured the Temple in Jerusalem was one of utter
desolation. The gates had been destroyed by fire. The court-
yard was overgrown with weeds. The buildings were in ruins,
the sanctuary polluted. There was no continual fire upon
the altar, for the sacrifices had ceased. The menorah had gone
out, and its perpetual light had ceased in the holy place. Most
of the priests had fled the city, as had Mattathias and his sons
many months earlier. The high priest at that time, the hellenizer Menelaus, also had abandoned whatever worship he had
been practicing in the Temple area.

The Temple was hushed and devastated. A wasteland.

The Maccabees "tore their garments, wailed loudly, put
ashes on their heads, and fell on their faces to the ground.
They sounded the ceremonial trumpets, and cried aloud to
Heaven" (1 Macc 4:39-40).

So desolate was the sanctuary, and so keenly were the Jews

aware of the hand of God in its reclamation, that they cried, "A great miracle has happened here." And they have continued this affirmation in the Hanukkah services ever since.

It was the seditious offensive of the Maccabees that ultimately delivered Judea out of the hands of King Antiochus and subsequently from all Seleucid control. Soon the Jews would have their own kings on the throne again. However, they would be Hasmoneans and not of the house of David.

The Temple also was recovered. Judas chose blameless priests to cleanse the sanctuary and to carry out the desecrated stones. They pulled down the defiled altar of burnt offerings where swine's blood had flowed. They piled up the polluted stones where the abomination of desolation had sat, to await the time when a prophet should come and tell them what to do with them. The altar was rebuilt and new vessels made. A new menorah, a new altar of incense, and a new table of shewbread also were constructed and returned to the holy place. Since the Ark of the Covenant was not in Zerubbabel's Temple, there is no mention of it in the renovated Temple either.

> Then, early on the twenty-fifth day of the ninth month, the month Kislev, in the year 148 [165 B.C.], sacrifice was offered as the law commands on the newly made altar of burnt-offering. On the anniversary of the day when the Gentiles had profaned it, on that very day, it was rededicated, with hymns of thanksgiving, to the music of harps and lutes and cymbals (1 Macc 4:52-54).

THE SURVIVAL OF THE JEWS

> And some of them that are wise shall fall, to refine them, and to purify, and to make them white, even to the time of the end; because it is yet for the time appointed (Dan 11:35).

Professor Jestrow was a distinguished faculty member of Yale University. Even though he was an American Jew, his life was in jeopardy for he was residing in Europe on the eve of World War II. He reflects upon the fate of European Jewry:

> Young people—young Americans especially—aren't aware that the tolerance for Jews in Europe is only fifty to a hundred years old and that it's never gone deep. It didn't touch Poland, where I was born. Even in the West—what about the Dreyfus case? No, no. In that respect Hitler represents only a return to normalcy for Europe, after a brief glow of liberation. The hostility simply moved from the Church to the anti-Semitic parties, because the French Revolution changed Europe from a religious to a political continent. If Hitler does win out, the Jews will fall back to the second-class status they always had under the kings and popes. Well, we survived seventeen centuries of that. We have a lot of wisdom and doctrine for coping with it.[3]

The centuries of pogroms which the Jews have experienced, beginning with Antiochus IV Epiphanes and running through the Nazi holocaust, demonstrate the unique capacity of the Jews, as a people, to survive. The Scriptures indicate that they will continue until the last great persecution under the Antichrist. The Jews will endure that holocaust also, but then their survival will terminate in glory rather than in despair, for that terminal persecution will prepare them to receive the Lord Jesus Christ as their Messiah.

The assurance of continuance is also reflected in Hanukkah. Today the observance of Hanukkah is rather standardized in Jewish homes. However, there was a time when a great debate raged over the order of lighting the Hanukkah candles. In the days of the Talmud, the school of Shammai insisted that all eight candles be lighted on the first night and then successively reduced until a lone candle burned on the last night. This reflected Shammai's belief that the Jewish spirit is to diminish throughout history until it is no more. He believed that Israel's best times are in the past.

3. Herman Wouk, *The Winds of War*, p. 30.

An opposite approach was taken by the school of Hillel. One candle should be lighted on the first night, leading up to the lighting of all eight on the last night of the festival of Hanukkah. Hillel's view prevailed, for he was optimistic about the survival of the Jewish people. Their best times lie in the future.

The New Testament teaches that the Jews will survive all threats of the Gentiles until the end days usher in the Messianic Kingdom and a faithful remnant of Jews will accept the Lord Jesus Christ as their Messiah King (Rom 11:25-27).

Rabbi Isaac Meir was a latter-day Hasidic who explained the difference between the two non-Mosaic feasts, Hanukkah and Purim. He said, "On Purim we celebrate the annulment of the royal edict to destroy the body; but on Hanukkah we were rescued from the decree which would have destroyed our souls."[4]

The Jews of Antiochus's day survived the physical threat of annihilation, as did their forefathers in the time of Queen Esther. But, in addition, they also overcame Hellenism's sophisticated threat to the spirit of Judaism. The rallying point was the Temple. It was the reclamation of the Temple on the first Hanukkah which symbolized the vitality and persistence of the covenant people Israel.

Reflecting this survival syndrome, the rabbis relate this story:

Once, while Moses was grazing his flock in the wilderness, he came to Mount Horeb. There he saw a thorn bush whose branches were ugly and forbidding, full of briars. Sorrowfully, Moses realized the similarity between this bush and the people Israel, for they, too, are lowly, and all who see them shall shun them. As he mused sadly upon the bush and the suffering of Israel, suddenly the bush burst into flame. Moses cried, "I have compared my people Israel to this bush when

---

4. Louis I. Newman, *The Hasidic Anthology*, p. 161.

out of it springs forth flames to consume it. O Lord God, must my people Israel perish?"

But when Moses saw how the bush was burned but not consumed, he rejoiced for he was made to realize the endurance of Israel when the voice of God said to him, "Even as this thorn bush is not consumed by the flame, so will the Jewish people survive all the flames of hate and persecution which are kindled against it. No evil or misfortune will be able to destroy Israel."

The dual threat of physical genocide and spiritual apostasy which intimidated the Jews during the Antiochus crisis is to emerge again in its most terrifying and virulent form during the reign of the Antichrist. However, the endurance of the Jews during the tribulational microcosm of Antiochus's day is a rehearsal for the survival of the Jews, both physically and spiritually, in the end days. Just as the Jews overcame the physical threats of Antiochus and the spiritual menace of Hellenism, so will the Jews of the Antichrist's reign survive the dual threat of that time, emerging as a purged and refined people, ready to receive the Messiah, the Lord Jesus Christ, when He comes in glory to reckon this national deliverance upon Israel which the prophet Daniel envisioned. Daniel viewed the persecution of the Antiochus crisis as prefiguring the Antichrist's persecution of the Jews in the end days, for both are as the refiners' fires which are "to refine them, and to purify, and to make them white, even to the time of the end; because it is yet for the time appointed" (Dan 11:35).

The Conflict Between Hellenist and Hasidim

And they that are wise among the people shall instruct many; yet they shall fall by the sword and by flame, by captivity and by spoil, many days (Dan 11:33).

The prophet Daniel mentions three groups of Jews who were significant in the Antiochus crisis. First, there were "such as do wickedly against the covenant" (11:32). These were the hellenizers whom we have already considered.

Second, there were the "many [who] shall join themselves unto them with flatteries" (11:34). These were Jews who were ready to go either way in their allegiance, depending upon whether the Hasidim or the Hellenists were prevailing. These vacillating Jews were fearful of Judas and his revolutionaries, and therefore they joined the revolt. Maccabean intolerance of those Jews who would not declare themselves for the covenant was notorious (1 Macc 3:5a, 8; 6:21-27; 7:5-7; 9:23).

"Now that they had an organized force, they turned their wrath on the guilty men and renegades. Those who escaped their fierce attacks took refuge with the Gentiles" (1 Macc 2:44). The Maccabees' fierce reprisals against those who had obeyed Antiochus's evil decrees caused others of those compromising Jews to turn to the Maccabean insurrectionists "with flatteries," said Daniel, in order to escape their wrath.

The third group of Jews to be identified by the prophet were those "that are wise among the people [who] shall instruct many. And some of them that are wise shall fall" (Dan 11:33a, 35a). These whom Daniel called the "wise" were subsequently known as Hasidim. "It was then that they [the Maccabees] were joined by a company of Hasidaeans, stalwarts of Israel, every one of them a volunteer in the cause of the law; and all who were refugees from the troubles came to swell their numbers, and so add to their strength" (1 Macc 2:42-43). Soon after the uprising at Modin and the beginning of the revolt, these Hasidim declared themselves on the side of the insurgents.

Hasidim is the plural form of a Hebrew word, *hasid*, which means "the pious ones." The term is now used in Judaism to refer to a mystical sect which was founded in the middle of the eighteenth century by a Ukrainian rabbi, Israel Baal Shem Tov. Hasidic groups remain today. They are most famous as the Naturei Karta, the ultrapietistic sect of Jews who live in the Mea-Shearim section of Jerusalem and who protest the new State of Israel because of its Messianic presumptions.[5]

Today's group is not to be confused with the Hasidim who joined the Maccabeans' rebellion against Antiochus IV Epiphanes. The latter group is the forerunner of the Pharisaical zealots of the New Testament.

Zeal for the Law became a part of Jewish piety, resulting from the persecutions of Antiochus. The Antiochus crisis served to radicalize Jewish piety and turn it into the aggressive fanaticism which was to characterize the Jewish Zealot from that day until the Great Revolt. The Hasidic movement has a long history extending back to the early Greek period and possibly further back into the Persian period. However, these groups of superpietistic enthusiasts suddenly came to light in the period of Antiochus's persecutions. The Hasidim were made up mostly of the poorer class, those from country villages, in contrast to the godless rich in Jerusalem. There were exceptions, of course, for Hasidim's leader in the early part of this era was the orthodox high priest, Onias III.

With their fierce zeal for the Law and their intolerance of those Jews who had compromised the covenant out of deference to the evil decrees of Antiochus, they joined the Maccabean party and swelled the ranks of the revolt with an enthusiasm which amounted to fierce fanaticism. Much of the success of the revolt was due to the vitality of the Hasidim, directed by the military genius of Judas Maccabee.

Daniel viewed their participation in the revolt, noting their wisdom, their concern for the priority of the Law (Dan 11:33a); their sacrifice, for "they shall fall by the sword and by flame, by captivity and by spoil, many days" (Dan 11:33b); and their inspiring example, for they "that are wise shall fall, to refine them, and to purify, and to make them white, even to the time of the end" (Dan 11:35).

5. Walter K. Price, *The Coming Antichrist*, pp. 45, 96.

The Coming of the Great Deliverer

Now when they shall fall, they shall be helped with a little help (Dan 11:34).

The suffering and survival of the Jews in Antiochus's day climaxed in the rise of Israel's great deliverer, Judas Maccabee. So the suffering and survival of the Jews in the Antichrist's day will climax in the advent of Israel's greatest Deliverer, the Lord Jesus Christ.

Actually there was not just one great deliverer of the Jews during the Antiochus crisis; there were five or six. The idea is embodied in the person of the old priest, Mattathias, along with his five sons. All of these heroes are personified by the one name which was given to Judas but which was subsequently applied to all—"Maccabees."

In addition, the idea of the hero dying for the deliverance of the people is also inherent in the Maccabean deliverance, for not a single one of the five sons died a natural death. Two of the brothers died on the field of battle under circumstances of exceptional gallantry, another was ambushed, a fourth was put to death in cold blood, while the fifth son was murdered. Therefore, in these Hasmoneans there was united the idea of the glorious deliverer who dies for the deliverance of the people.

The same idea reappears in the Jewish concept of the Messiah, for the rabbis in the Talmud and Midrash speak of Messiah Ben Joseph, who died for the people; and of Messiah Ben David, who is to be the glorious reigning messiah.

So the great Deliverer who will lead Israel into national deliverance in the end days, the Lord Jesus Christ, has also died that the great deliverance might take place. The obvious difference between Jesus the Messiah and Judas the Maccabee is that Judas delivered the people and then died, while Jesus died first, then He will deliver the people, having arisen from the grave and ascended into heaven, from whence He will come again.

Many believe that Psalms 44 and 74 have a postexilic authorship and may have been written during the Antiochus crisis. These two psalms express Israel's hope of deliverance from the devastation caused by Antiochus IV Epiphanes. Their words also will be remembered by the Jews in the end days during the Great Tribulation period in anticipation of the coming Messiah, the great Deliverer of Israel.

> They have set thy sanctuary
>   on fire;
> They have profaned the
>   dwelling-place of thy name
>   by casting it to the ground.
> They said in their heart, Let
>   us make havoc of them alto-
>   gether:
> They have burned up all the
>   synagogues of God in the land.
> We see not our signs:
> There is no more any
>   prophet;
> Neither is there among us any
>   that knoweth how long.
> How long, O God, shall the
>   adversary reproach?
> Shall the enemy blaspheme
>   thy name for ever?
> Why drawest thou back thy
>   hand, even thy right hand?
> Pluck it out of thy bosom
>   and consume them.
>
>   PSALM 74:7-11

The New Testament has the answer to the question which the ancient psalmist was asking during the time of Antiochus's persecutions.

For I would not, brethren, have you ignorant of this mystery, lest ye be wise in your own conceits, that a hardening in part hath befallen Israel, until the fulness of the Gentiles be come in; and so all Israel shall be saved: even as it is written,

There shall come out of Zion
the Deliverer;
He shall turn away ungodli-
ness from Jacob:
And this is my covenant
unto them,
When I shall take away their
sins.

ROMANS 11:25-27

9

The End of Days: The Coming Antichrist

Daniel 11:36-45

Fulfillment: The End of Days

DANIEL 11:36 is the point in our text where the faulty interpretation of the liberal critic really begins to reveal itself. Prior to this point in Daniel 11, the a priori assumptions of the higher critic insists that these verses were written by a pseudonymous Daniel who actually lived during the Maccabean era. Writing of events which had already taken place under the guise of predictive prophecy, the higher critics maintain that it is obvious that this forgery could "predict" with great precision the events which already had happened.

With Daniel 11:36 an additional question emerges: Is Antiochus IV Epiphanes still the subject of these verses? Does Daniel 11:36-39 characterize King Antiochus? If so, then this portrayal of him cannot be substantiated by the ancient sources which have so concisely verified the preceding verses. Furthermore, the events of Daniel 11:40-45 are absolutely impossible to apply to the final days of King Antiochus, for he did not die in Judea between the coast and Jerusalem as a result of renewed hostilities with Egypt, the way these verses would indicate if they were applied to him. It is a fact of history that Antiochus died in Persia.[1]

As a result of holding to the late date of Daniel, some critics theorize that this is how the Jews in general, and the unknown

1. Polybius *Histories* 31.11.

writer of Daniel in particular, assumed that Antiochus IV
Epiphanes should meet his just fate. "Our text implies that
Antiochus died in Palestine between the Mediterranean and
Mount Zion," says Professor Charles, "whereas he actually
died at Tabae in Persia, 164 B.C. It was a reasonable expecta-
tion on the part of the Jews, that their greatest persecutor
should fall amid the scenes of his greatest crimes."[2] A more
radical critic would simply dismiss this as prophecy gone
astray, for in these verses this Maccabean Daniel quit recording history and attempted to predict the future. He failed.

However, the problem disappears when we recognize that
Daniel's vision now transcends the second-century B.C. reign
of King Antiochus and reaches into the far distant future.
Previously Daniel had been depicting the events of King
Antiochus's day (11:21-35), but now his prophecy merges into
a description of Antiochus's successor, the Gentile world dictator whose malevolent reign will occur during the end days
(11:36-45). Particularly does Daniel anticipate the spiritual
motivation of the Antichrist (11:36-39), as well as predicting
the military movements which will lead ultimately to his destruction (11:40-45).

Thus Daniel 11:36-45 is prophecy yet to find fulfillment
during the time of Jewish anguish which will fill the interim
between the disappearance of the Church (1 Thess 4:13-18)
and the second coming of Christ (Rev 19:11-16). The duration of this interval between the two phases of the Lord's
return is assumed to be seven years, paralleling the seventieth
week of Daniel's great time prophecy found in 9:24-27. During
this time the Antichrist will ascend to the throne of world
dominion. As a benevolent dictator he will favor the Jews,
allowing them to revive their ancient Levitical system of worship. The Temple will also be rebuilt during this climactic
period of Jewish history.

Becoming firmly established in his world empire, the Anti-

2. R. H. Charles, *The Book of Daniel,* in The Century Bible, 11:138.

christ will then aspire to be worshiped as God. The remaining three and one half years of this period will be given over to the terrorizing attempts of the Antichrist to force a contemporary Hellenism, the cult of the beast, upon the Jews. The oppression of the Great Tribulation is prefigured by Antiochus's cruel reign. During the final epoch many Jews will compromise their allegiance to the covenant God of Israel and receive the mark of the beast. Others—a faithful remnant in Israel—will retain their orthodox commitment to Yahweh. These are they who will be purged by this ultimate holocaust and made ready to receive the Lord Jesus Christ as their Messiah when He comes in glory (Zech 12:10; 13:1; Rom 11:25-27).

In our text, therefore, Daniel is not depicting the death of King Antiochus Epiphanes but the final destiny of the Antichrist (Dan 11:40-45) ; and a fate which was predetermined by his blasphemous attitude toward the God of Israel (Dan 11:36-39).

ANTICHRIST'S BLASPHEMOUS ATTITUDE WHICH WILL DETERMINE HIS ULTIMATE DEMISE

And the king shall do according to his will; and he shall exalt himself, and magnify himself above every god, and shall speak marvelous things against the God of gods; and he shall prosper till the indignation be accomplished; for that which is determined shall be done. Neither shall he regard the gods of his father, nor the desire of women, nor regard any god; for he shall magnify himself above all. But in his place shall he honor the god of fortresses; and a god whom his fathers knew not shall he honor with gold, and silver, and with precious stones, and the pleasant things. And he shall deal with the strongest fortresses by the help of a foreign god: whosoever acknowledgeth him he will increase with glory; and he shall cause them to rule over many, and shall divide the land for a price (Dan 11:36-39).

Antiochus IV Epiphanes claimed to be "God Manifest." Yet, paradoxically, he was a religious person who revered deity other than himself. Apparently he was an Epicurean in religious matters. He had been personally converted to this philosophy by Philonides who, for a while, operated a school in Antioch.[3]

There is some evidence that Antiochus was influenced by demonic powers also. Not only do his erratic behavior and his diabolical cruelty give empirical evidence of this, but there is also tangible evidence which may still be seen in his capital of Antioch.

The only surviving monument of the Antiochus era is an image carved on the mountainside high above Antioch. The figure is that of a veiled head. On the right shoulder stands another figure—now greatly weathered—with a basket on its head. The people of the city called this figure the "Charonian." The story is that a seer named Leios instructed that a great mask be carved upon the mountainside in order to appease the gods of the underworld and bring an end to a devastating plague which was causing terrible suffering. "And inscribing something on it he [Antiochus] put an end to the pestilential death," says Malalas.[4] What this inscription might have been which King Antiochus carved on this figure we do not know, for the bust is badly chipped and part of the chest is missing. Some scholars who have studied this monument believe that the name "Charonian" refers to an underworld deity who was appeased, thus ending the plague which had sent many souls to Charon, a ferryman who conveyed the souls of the dead across the Styx to the abode of the god of hell, according to Greek mythology.

Whatever the meaning of this monument might have been, it is sufficiently evident that King Antiochus was religious, having reverence for both good and evil spirits.

3. Martin Hengel, *Judaism and Hellenism*, 1:86.
4. Malalas *Chronicle of John Malalas* 205:8-13; in Matthew Spinka and Glanville Downey, trans., *Chronicle of John Malalas*, p. 16.

The Antichrist will also be a religious person. However, his gods are far different from the God of the Jews or the Saviour of the saints whom he will persecute during the Great Tribulation period.

In Daniel 11:36-39, "god" is mentioned eight times. The Antichrist will magnify himself "above every god," indicating that he will believe in many gods, while subordinating all of them to his own person. His disregard for the "God of gods" will be exemplified by his speaking awesome things against Him. He will have no "regard [for] the gods of his fathers," nor will he "regard any god," for that matter. He will "honor the god of fortresses," "a god whom his fathers knew not." He will subdue the strongest fortress by the aid of this "foreign god."

This was Daniel's estimation of the spiritual motivation of the Antichrist. He will not be an irreligious person, for he will be aware of many gods. Nevertheless, the Antichrist will exalt himself above them all.

If any deity will be revered by the Antichrist it will be the "god of fortresses." Who is this "god of fortresses"? We must return to King Antiochus for background material which will reflect an answer to this question.

There is some evidence that Antiochus was especially devoted to the Roman god of war[5] who had a counterpart in the Greek Pantheon. Mars's counterpart is known as Ares, son of Zeus. Greek mythology says that Ares had two sons, Deimos and Phobos, gods of terror and tumult. Ares is also related to Enyo, goddess of battle, and to Eris, goddess of discord. The vulture and the dog, scavengers of the battlefield, are Ares' favorite pets.

Antiochus expanded Antioch by building a new suburb called "Epiphaneia." He constructed a magnificent temple of Jupiter Capitolinus there.[6] Apparently this new temple was

5. Judah J. Slotki, *Daniel, Ezra, Nehemiah*, p. 98.
6. Livy *The History of Rome* 41.20.

a replica of the one in Rome, for he had been greatly impressed by the Roman gods while a hostage there. This temple, still unfinished at his death, was completed years later by Tiberius. It was probably designed by the famous Roman architect, Cossutius. His name has been found scratched in the cement walls of an aqueduct which he also designed for Antiochus in Antioch, indicating that he was working in the city. Professor Bouchier of Oxford theorizes that this temple represents Antiochus's break with the Greek gods of his Seleucid fathers and the establishment of the worship of the Roman gods in Antioch. He says,

> On the upper part of the Acropolis hill [in Epiphaneis] rose a temple of Jupiter Capitolinus, a compliment to the republic [of Roma] which Antiochus felt bound to propitiate. This building had a gilt ceiling, the whole inside walls were covered with gold plates, and it probably contained a statue of Rome herself with a murial crown. Some such alien figure impressed itself on the imagination of the prophet Daniel, who saw in his vision Antiochus honouring, in place of the god of his fathers, "the god of fortress and a god whom his fathers knew not."[7]

Antiochus's devotion to the gods of warfare is also indicated by the ancient sources. He introduced the depraved Roman sport of gladiatorial combat into Antioch, repulsing its citizens until they finally became used to its cruelty and carnage. Livy says that the king "kindled in the young men a passion for arms."[8]

The "god of fortress" whom Antichrist is said to honor seems to be a personification of this battle psychology which also was apparent in his prototype, Antiochus IV Epiphanes. The Antichrist's religion will be steel dripping with blood. His devotion will be to belligerence and violence. His spirit

7. E. S. Bouchier, *A Short History of Antioch, 300 B.C. to A.D. 1268*, pp. 34-35.
8. Livy, 41.20.

will be that of Mars, god of war. His will be an ethic of military victory whose highest good will be suffering, destruction, and death. This is the essence of the "god of fortresses" who is the spiritual mentor of the Antichrist.

This may be Daniel's way of stating what the book of the Revelation is later to affirm, namely, that the Antichrist is inspired by Satan and moves at his malevolent behest (Rev 13:4). Therefore the violence and carnage of war are a proper frame of reference by which to characterize the Antichrist and his diabolical motivation.

The first act of Satan, after he was liberated from his allegiance to God, who created him, was to enter into war with the angels of heaven (Rev 12:7-8). One of his last acts on earth will be to war with the saints of God, particularly with the nation Israel, through his emissary, the Antichrist.

Seemingly the Antichrist will thrive in this aura of violence, for Daniel decreed that "he shall prosper." However, his days are numbered. He will flourish "till the indignation be accomplished," said Daniel. "Indignation" is that time under God's appointment in which He will work out His purposes—largely through suffering—for His covenant people Israel (cf. Dan 8:19). This term is used by Isaiah in reference to the Exile (Isa 10:5, 25), a time of indignation upon Israel which purged them of idolatry. The Great Tribulation period will be God's appointed time of indignation to purge Israel of her rebellion and prepare the covenant people to receive the Lord Jesus Christ as Messiah. During this indignation, God's instrument will be the sadistic and inhuman atrocities of the Antichrist whose persecution of the Jews will ready them for the advent of the Messiah and the establishment of the golden age. "For that which is determined shall be done," said Daniel (11:36b).

THE TERMINATION OF THE REIGN OF THE ANTICHRIST

And at the time of the end shall the king of the south

contend with him; and the king of the north shall come against him like a whirlwind, with chariots, and with horsemen, and with many ships; and he shall enter into the countries, and shall overflow and pass through. He shall enter also into the glorious land, and many countries shall be overthrown; but these shall be delivered out of his hand: Edom, and Moab, and the chief of the children of Ammon. He shall stretch forth his hand also upon the countries; and the land of Egypt shall not escape. But he shall have power over the treasures of gold and of silver, and over all the precious things of Egypt; and the Libyans and the Ethiopians shall be at his steps. But tidings out of the east and out of the north shall trouble him; and he shall go forth with great fury to destroy and utterly to sweep away many. And he shall plant the tents of his palace between the sea and the glorious holy mountain; yet he shall come to his end, and none shall help him (Dan 11:40-45).

Jesus said, "All they that take the sword shall perish with the sword" (Matt 26:52). The Antichrist will worship the "god of fortresses" whose ethic is conquest, enslavement, and destruction. He then will come to his appointed end in a great military carnage.

Once again, it is obvious that this passage cannot refer to King Antiochus IV Epiphanes, for it declares that both the king of the south and the king of the north come against the king who is the subject of these verses. Furthermore, Daniel specifies "the time of the end" as the context of this military invasion.

It is generally agreed that the Antichrist will be involved in three distinct military operations during the seventieth week of Daniel.

First, there will be the military conflict in which the three nations will be subdued and the ten-nation confederation, which will comprise the revived Roman Empire, will emerge. This will occur during the first part of the seventieth week.

Daniel was aware of the Antichrist's devotion to the "god of
fortresses," which will result in his irresistible conquest of "the
strongest fortresses by the help of a foreign god" (11:39). This
may reflect the Antichrist's victory over the nations early in
the seventieth week, which will reestablish the ancient Roman
Empire.

Second, apparently there will be another conflict involving
the foe from the far north (Russia?), along with some allies in
the south (Ezek 38:1-6) who will oppose the Antichrist. The
scene of the conflagration will be the land of Israel. The time
will be toward the middle of the seventieth week, or just before the three-and-one-half-year Great Tribulation begins.
The foe from the far north will be subdued. This invasion of
Israel by the foe from the far north, and the subsequent battle
between the foe and the forces of the Antichrist who will happen to be in Israel, seem to be the subjects of Daniel 11:40-45.
In these verses the king of the north (Russia, perhaps, which
is now the dominant empire in the north, just as the Seleucid
Empire was the dominant empire in the north during the
second century B.C.) and the king of the south (still Egypt)
will "contend with him," that is, the Antichrist. Never before
have the king of the north and the king of the south been
allied as they will be at that time.

If the events of this prophecy were to be fulfilled in our
day, then an alliance between Russia and the Arab countries
would be the frame of reference. But no matter when it does
occur, something similar to an alliance between Russia and
the Arabs was predicted by Daniel. However, these allies,
whoever they might be in the future, will be defeated by the
Antichrist. Only Edom, Moab, and Ammon will be exempted
from this sweeping conquest. Perhaps the people who inhabit
these ancient territories will be divinely preserved in order
that they might provide shelter for the fleeing Jews during the
ensuing persecution which will be about to descend upon
Israel from the Antichrist.

It will be during the military engagement just before the Great Tribulation begins, in which the king of the north will be allied with the king of the south against the Antichrist, that he (the Antichrist) will receive the death wound from which he will miraculously recover (Rev 13:3, 12, 14). Antiochus IV Epiphanes was rumored dead, but he was not. He returned to Jerusalem, issued his evil decrees, and the world's first religious persecution began. The Antichrist will also be (rumored?) dead, but will be alive again. He will also descend upon Israel and impose history's final religious persecution upon the Jews.

This is the Great Tribulation which was predicted by Jesus in Matthew 24:15-28. Daniel also made reference to this era of intense suffering in 12:1-2.

The reasons for the Great Tribulation will be spiritual. The Antichrist will be determined that the world should worship him as God. The Jews will be the arch-resisters of his designs, just as they were in the second century B.C. when Antiochus IV Epiphanes desired to be worshiped as God. Consequently, the Antichrist will severely persecute the Jews, as did King Antiochus, in order to force them to worship him.

However, God also has a purpose for the Great Tribulation. He will use these days of unprecedented suffering to prepare the Jews to receive Jesus as the Messiah. The Church has already done what the Great Tribulation is designed to do for the Jews, namely, lead them to accept Jesus Christ as Saviour and Messiah. Therefore, the Church does not appear in the Great Tribulation. It will be taken out of the world just prior to the beginning of Daniel's seventieth week.

There will be a third military conflict, which we believe to be depicted in Daniel 11:44-45, in which the Antichrist will meet his end. The place where his demise will occur is in Israel, "between the sea and the glorious holy mountain," that is, between the Mediterranean coast and Mount Zion.

Antiochus IV Epiphanes died in 164 B.C., but not in Israel.

He was in Persia at the time of his death. Our ancient sources attribute the death of Antiochus to his sacrilege and blasphemy. The ancient historians believed that King Antiochus died because

> he not only opposed the god of Judea but also, inflamed by the fires of avarice, tried to despoil the temple of Artemis, which was very rich, in Elymais. . . . He was driven mad by certain apparitions and terrors, and finally died of disease, and they [Polybius and Diodorus] state that this happened to him because he attempted to violate the temple of Artemis.[9]

Polybius says that Antiochus "died in the course of his return at Tabae, in Persia, driven mad, as some say, by some manifestations of divine wrath in the course of his wicked attempt upon this temple."[10]

King Antiochus was not even afforded a royal burial, according to Granius Licinnanius. A translation of his epitaph reads something like this: "His body, while it was being carried to Antioch, snatched away in the river, when the beasts of burden were suddenly frightened, was not visible."[11] Apparently his body fell from a wagon when the animals pulling it became frightened, while fording a body of water. The corpse disappeared. No tomb marks the burial place of Antiochus IV Epiphanes.

The Antichrist will also meet his end as a result of defaming the God of Israel. This is why Daniel placed the Antichrist's profane worship (11:36-39) in juxtaposition to his destruction (11:40-45). The Antichrist obviously will meet his fatal end because of his blasphemy of the God of Israel, just as the an-

9. Diodorus Siculus *Library of History* 31.18.
10. Polybius, 31.11.
11. Granius Licinianus *Liber* 28; cf. Barry Phillips, "Antiochus IV Epiphanes," *Journal of Biblical Literature* 29 (1910): 138 n. Also see Edwyn R. Bevan, "A Note on Antiochus Epiphanes," *The Journal of Hellenic Studies* 20 (1900): 26.

cients believed that King Antiochus met his just fate for similar sacrileges.

Furthermore, King Antiochus's body disappeared when his hearse overturned while crossing a river. No funeral was held. No tomb commemorates his exit from this life. In a similar way the Antichrist will not be buried. No tomb will mark the end of his career, for he will be "cast alive into the lake of fire that burneth with brimstone" (Rev 19:20b). Along with the false prophet and the devil, the Antichrist will "be tormented day and night for ever and ever" (20:10b).

An interesting final parallel exists between these two Gentile terrorizers of the Jews. Antiochus Epiphanes disappeared in a lake of water while the Antichrist will disappear in a lake of fire.

Daniel depicts the circumstances which will surround the final destruction of the Antichrist in 11:44-45.

A previous invasion from the north will have been repulsed by the Antichrist. Then renewed "tidings out of the east and out of the north shall trouble him" (v. 44). These tidings will be the prelude to the Battle of Armageddon which will bring to a close the career of the Antichrist and terminate the Great Tribulation period with the second coming of Christ.

Revelation 16:12 indicates that one of the belligerents in the final battle will be "the kings that come from the sunrising," the Far East. The advent of these Oriental forces will be the "tidings out of the east" of which Daniel speaks. These tidings will spread down from "the north" also, says Daniel.

Why will they come from both directions?

All invasions of Israel have come from either the north or the south. Israel's eastern border was protected by the desert, as the west was protected by the sea. These kings from the sunrising, the Far East, will cross the Euphrates River, which will be dried up for their advent (Rev 16:12), go around the Fertile Crescent, and invade Israel from the north. Hence, the "tidings out of the east and out of the north [which] shall trouble" the Antichrist.

They will engage the forces of the Antichrist who will happen to be in the land. The conflict will begin on the vast Plain of Esdraelon in Galilee, below the ancient fortress of Megiddo (Rev 16:16), and will terminate in the city of Jerusalem (Joel 3:1-2, 12; Zech 14:1-3). The Antichrist will meet his doom sometime during these battles. Daniel says that it will occur somewhere in the Shephelah or on the Plain of Sharon, between Jerusalem and the Mediterranean.

He will not be killed, for he will be "cast *alive* into the lake of fire" (Rev 19:20, itals. added). His demise will occur in the context of the second coming of Christ. At this point he will be summarily swept into oblivion by the Lord Jesus who will descend to earth in great glory "with the angels of his power in flaming fire, rendering vengeance to them that know not God, and to them that obey not the gospel of our Lord Jesus: who shall suffer punishment, even eternal destruction from the face of the Lord and from the glory of his might, when he shall come to be glorified in his saints, and to be marvelled at in all them that believed . . . in that day" (2 Thess 1:7-10).

Israel will be delivered and the Messiah, the Lord Jesus Christ whom Israel will accept, will establish His Kingdom on earth.

During the glorious aftermath of the Six-Day War in 1967, Leon Uris wrote:

> I have seen miracles. From the lowest point in our history, we Jews have risen to the highest point in our history in a mere twenty-five years. From the Holocaust of World War II to the victorious battles for freedom in Israel. The world has seen the last generation of Jews to ever go to their deaths without fighting . . . so they fought three wars for freedom in two decades. In the end, the Jews stood alone. As in the beginning they were few but they were brave. And they crushed the enemies all around them with such swiftness

that all men in all places stood in awe. It did not seem that this was an army of mortals. And the terrible odyssey was over. Never again would the Jews have to wail in anguish, "Next Year In Jerusalem." . . . And when the third and final war was done they went up into their ancient capital. Many of them had dropped the names of their exile and taken ancient names. Ben-Gurion and Dayan and Rabin and Meir and Eban. And they stood before the Western Wall of the Temple and prayed and danced and they wept for joy. And the Lord felt they had kept the faith well and suffered enough. And he bade them build a third Temple and dwell in their own land, forever.[12]

This famous novelist's vision is premature. Israel will not dwell in the land forever—secure around the third Temple—until another war, the final war of Armageddon, is fought and permanent peace is ushered in by the coming of the Messiah.

After the death of Antiochus IV Epiphanes in 164 B.C., the issues in Judea were altered. Formally, the concern of the insurgents was spiritual survival. However, the next years were characterized by a new nationalism whose concern was the reclamation of political independence and the reestablishment of an autonomous state, independent from Seleucid encroachment and self-determined, under the leadership of their own kings. For the first time since the Exile, a movement for complete independence developed among the Jews. The political independence of Judah was not actually realized until some thirty years after the death of King Antiochus IV Epiphanes when the Seleucid Empire fell to pieces, broken by civil strife. And it was not until 104 B.C. that Aristobulus, a Hasmonean, dared to actually call himself "king." Nevertheless, it was the Maccabean revolt and the death of King Antiochus which made possible the ultimate independence of the Jews—for a while.

12. Excerpt from "The Third Temple"; copyright © 1967 by Leon Uris, appears in *Strike Zion* by William Stephenson, published by Bantam Books, Inc. Used by permission.

Similarly, it is the destruction of the Antichrist and the accession of the Lord Jesus Christ, Israel's Messiah, to the throne, thus ushering in the Kingdom age, which was envisioned by all the prophets of Israel who looked forward to this golden age.

Abba Eban says,

> Other people have dreamed of a golden age in which the conflict between security and freedom is transcended but all pre-Jewish civilizations place their golden age in the past—at the beginning of history—so that human life appears as a constant descent from an ancient felicity. Judaism also had the genius to see the era of perfection as lying in the future—at the end of days—so that all history appears to unfold in progress—forward and upward—towards ascending goals. This belief in the positive direction of human history, is characteristically, and unequivocally, and originally Hebrew.[13]

This glorious dream of the prophets of Israel for a golden age will be fulfilled at the second coming of Christ.

---

13. Abba Eban, *The Meaning of Jewish History*, p. 13.

Appendix I

The Ptolemaic Empire (Egypt)

Ptolemy I Soter	305-285 B.C.
Ptolemy II Philadelphus	285-246 B.C.
Ptolemy III Euergetes	246-221 B.C.
Ptolemy IV Philopator	221-203 B.C.
Ptolemy V Epiphanes	203-180 B.C.
Ptolemy VI Philometor	180-145 B.C.
Ptolemy VII Euergetes II, Physcon	145-116 B.C.
Ptolemy VIII Soter II, Lathyros	116-108 B.C.
Ptolemy IX Alexander	108-88 B.C.
Ptolemy VIII Soter II, Lathyros	88-80 B.C.
Ptolemy X Alexander II	80 B.C.
Ptolemy XI Auletes	80-51 B.C.
Ptolemy XII and Cleopatra VII	51-48 B.C.
Ptolemy XIII and Cleopatra VII	47-44 B.C.
Ptolemy XIV (Caesar) and Cleopatra VII	44-30 B.C.

The Seleucid Empire (Syria)

Seleucus I Nicator	312-280 B.C.
Antiochus I Soter	280-262 B.C.
Antiochus II Theos	262-246 B.C.
Seleucus II Callinicus	246-226 B.C.
Seleucus III Ceraunus	226-223 B.C.
Antiochus III the Great	223-187 B.C.
Seleucus IV Philopator	187-175 B.C.
Antiochus IV Epiphanes	175-164 B.C.
Antiochus V Eupator	164-161 B.C.
Demetrius I Soter	161-150 B.C.
Alexander Balas	150-145 B.C.

Demetrius II Nicator	145-138	B.C.
Antiochus VI Epiphanes	145-142	B.C.
Tryphon	142-138	B.C.
Antiochus VII Euergetes, Sidetes	138-129	B.C.
Demetrius II Nicator	129-126	B.C.
Antiochus VIII Grypos	126-96	B.C.
Antiochus IX Kyzikenos	115-95	B.C.

(Confusion with rival claimants intensified for the next thirty years)

THE PERSIAN EMPIRE

Cyrus	538-529	B.C.
Cambyses	529-522	B.C.
Pseudo Smerdis	522	B.C.
Darius I Hystaspis	522-486	B.C.
Xerxes I	485-465	B.C.
Artaxerxes I Longimanus	464-424	B.C.
Xerxes II	424	B.C.
Darius II Nothus	423-404	B.C.
Artaxerxes II Mnemon	404-459	B.C.
Artaxerxes III Ochus	359-338	B.C.
Darius III Codomannus	338-331	B.C.

THE HASMONAEANS

Judas Maccabee	165-160	B.C.
Jonathan (high priest)	160-142	B.C.
Simon (high priest)	142-134	B.C.
John Hyrcanus I (high priest)	134-104	B.C.
Aristobulus I (high priest, king)	103	B.C.
Alexander Jannaeus (high priest, king)	102-75	B.C.
Alexandra Salome	75-66	B.C.
Hyrcanus II (high priest)	75-66	B.C.
Aristobulus II (high priest, king)	66-63	B.C.
Hyrcanus II (high priest)	63-40	B.C.
Antigonus (high priest, king)	40-37	B.C.
Herod the Great	37-4	B.C.

Appendix II

Daniel	Date Fulfilled	The Reign in Which Fulfilled
11:2	550-465 B.C.	Persian kings: Cambyses, Pseudo-Smerdis, Darius I, Xerxes I
11:3	334-323 B.C.	Alexander the Great of Macedonia
11:4	321-301 B.C.	The Diadochi: Ptolemy I, Seleucus I, Cassander, Lysimachus
11:5	321-280 B.C.	Ptolemy I Soter of Egypt Seleucus I Nicator of Syria
11:6	249-246 B.C.	Ptolemy II Philadelphus Antiochus II Theos
11:7-9	246-240 B.C.	Ptolemy III Euergetes Seleucus II Callinicus
11:10-19	226-187 B.C.	Ptolemy IV Philopator and Ptolemy V Epiphanes; Seleucus III Ceraunus and Antiochus III the Great
11:20	187-175 B.C.	Seleucus IV Philopator
11:21	175 B.C.	Antiochus IV Epiphanes' accession to the throne
11:22-24	175-170 B.C.	Judea during the first years of Antiochus's reign
11:25-28	169 B.C.	Antiochus's first Egyptian campaign and terror in Jerusalem

11:29-30	168 B.C.	Antiochus's second Egyptian campaign and terror in Jerusalem
11:31-32a	168-165 B.C.	Antiochus's evil decrees
11:32b-35	165 B.C.	Judas Maccabee, Judea's great deliverer
11:36-45	End Days	To be fulfilled during the reign of the Antichrist

Bibliography

ANCIENT LITERARY SOURCES

Aelian (Claudius Aelianus) *De natura animalium*.

———. *Varia historia*.

Appian of Alexandria. *Macedonica*.

———. *Syriaca*.

Athenaeus. *Deipnosophistai*.

Cicero. *Philippica*. 8.23.

Curtius, Rufus Quintus. *Acts of the Great Alexander*.

Diodorus Siculus. *Library of History*.

Granius Licinianus. *Liber*. 28.

St. Jerome (Hieronymous). *Commentary on Daniel*. Chap. 11.

Josephus, Flavius. *The Antiquities of the Jews*.

———. *Wars of the Jews*.

———. *Against Apion*.

Justinius Marcus. *History of the World*. Dublin: Dykes, 1724.

Libanius. *Oration*. 11.122-23.

Livy (Titus Livinus). *History of Rome*.

Malalas, John. *Chronicle of John Malalas*.

Midrash Rabbah. Soncino ed.

Pausanias. *Description of Greece*.

Pliny the Elder (Gaius Plinius Secundus). *Natural History*.

Polyaenus. *Strategemata*.

Polybius. *The Histories*.

Strabo. *Geography*.

Tacitus. *Histories*.

The Babylonian Talmud. Soncino ed.

Valerius Maximus. *Nine Books of Memorable Deeds and Sayings*.

Vegetius (Flavius Vegetius Renatus). *The Military Institutions of the Romans*.

Velleius Paterculus, Gaius. *Historiae Romanae Liber Primus— Secundus*.

OTHER SOURCES

Abbott, Jacob. *Histories of Cyrus the Great and Alexander the Great.* New York: Harper, 1880.

Archer, Gleason L. trans. *Jerome's Commentary on Daniel.* Grand Rapids: Baker, 1958.

Augus, Jacob Bernard. *The Meaning of Jewish History.* Vol. 1. London: Abelard-Schuman, 1963.

Badian, E., ed. *Studies in Greek and Roman History.* Oxford: Blackwell, 1964.

Baron, David. *A Divine Forecast of Jewish History.* London: Morgan & Scott, n.d.

Baron, Joseph. *A Social and Religious History of the Jews.* 13 vols. Philadelphia: Jewish Pubn. Soc., 1952.

Bartlett, John R. *The First and Second Books of the Maccabees.* Cambridge: Cambridge U., 1973.

Bentwich, Norman. *Hellenism.* Philadelphia: Jewish Pubn. Soc., 1919.

Bevan. A. *A Short Commentary on the Book of Daniel for the Use of Students.* Cambridge: Cambridge U., 1892.

Bevan, Edwyn R. *The House of Seleucus.* Vol. 8. London: Arnold, 1902.

———. *Jerusalem Under the High Priests.* London: Arnold, 1958.

———. "A Note on Antiochus Epiphanes," *The Journal of Hellenistic Studies* 20 (1900) :26-28.

———. "Syria and the Jews," in *The Cambridge Ancient History.* Vol. 8. Cambridge: Cambridge U., 1954.

Bickerman, Elias. *The Maccabees.* New York: Schocken, 1947.

Birnbaum, Philip. *A Book of Jewish Concepts.* New York: Hebrew Pubn., 1964.

Bloch, Sam E. *Holocaust and Rebirth.* Tel Aviv: Bergen Belsen, 1965.

Bouchier, E. S. *A Short History of Antioch, 300 B.C. to A.D. 1268.* Oxford: Blackwell, 1921.

Bousset, Wilhelm, *The Antichrist.* London: Hutchinson, 1896.

Box, G. H. *Judaism in the Greek Period.* Oxford: Clarendon, 1932.

Burich, Nancy J. *Alexander the Great: A Bibliography.* Kent, O.: Kent State U., 1970.

Burn, Andrew R. *Alexander the Great and the Hellenistic Empire*. London: Hodder & Stoughton, 1947.

Cary, Earnest, trans. *Dionysius of Halicarnassus' Roman Antiquities*. Cambridge, Mass.: Harvard U., 1937-50.

Cary, George. *The Medieval Alexander*. Cambridge: Cambridge U., 1955.

Cary, Max. *A History of the Greek World from 323-146 B.C.* London: Methuen, 1951.

Charles, R. H. *The Apocrypha and Pseudepigrapha of the Old Testament*. Vol. 2. Oxford: Clarendon, 1963.

———. *The Book of Daniel*. The Century Bible. Vol. 11. London: Caxton, n.d.

———. *A Critical and Exegetical Commentary on the Book of Daniel*. Oxford: Clarendon, 1929.

———. *Religion's Development Between the Old and New Testaments*. London: Butterworth, 1934.

Cohen, A. *The Soncino Chumash*. London: Soncino, 1971.

Cohen, Norman. *Warrant for Genocide*. New York: Harper & Row, 1967.

Cook, S. A.; Adcock, F. E.; and Charlesworth, M. P., eds. *The Cambridge Ancient History*. Vol. 8: "Rome and the Mediterranean 218-133 B.C." Cambridge: Cambridge U., 1954.

Criswell, W. A. *Expository Sermons on the Book of Daniel*. Grand Rapids: Zondervan, 1968.

Culver, Robert D. *Daniel and the Latter Days*. Chicago: Moody, 1954.

Cummings, Lewis V. *Alexander the Great*. Boston: Houghton Mifflin, 1940.

Curtius, Rufus Quintus. *The Acts of the Great Alexander*. New York: Da Capo, 1971.

Dagut, M. B. "II Maccabees and the Death of Antiochus IV Epiphanes," *The Journal of Biblical Literature* 72 (1953).

Daney, J. C. *A Commentary on I Maccabees*. Oxford: Blackwell, 1954.

Davis, W. Hersey, and McDowell, Edward A. *A Source Book of Interbiblical History*. Nashville: Broadman, 1948.

Dimont, Max I. *The Indestructible Jews*. New York: Norton, 1971.

———. *Jews, God and History*. New York: Signet, 1962.

Dinsmore, William B. "The Repair of the Athena Parthenos," *The American Journal of Archaeology* (1934).

Dobnov, Simon. *History of the Jews*. Vol. 1. London: Yoseloff, 1967.

Donat, Alexander. *The Holocaust Kingdom*. New York: Holt, Rinehart & Winston, 1965.

Downey, Glanville. *Ancient Antioch*. Princeton: Princeton U., 1963.

———. *A History of Antioch in Syria from Seleucus to the Arab Conquest*. Princeton: Princeton U., 1961.

Downey, Glanville, trans. "Libanius' Oration XI, 'In Praise of Antioch,'" *Proceedings of the American Philological Society* 103 (1959).

Driver, S. R. *The Book of Daniel*. Cambridge: Cambridge U., 1901.

Dryden, John, trans. *Plutarch: The Lives of the Noble Grecians and Romans*. New York: Modern Lib., n.d.

Eban, Abba. *The Meaning of Jewish History*. USA: Soc. of Jewish Bibliophiles, 1964.

———. *My Country*. New York: Random House, 1972.

———. *My People*. New York: Behrman, 1968.

Ehrenberg, Victor. *Alexander and the Greeks*. Oxford: Blackwell, 1938.

Emmrich, Kurt. *Alexander the Great; Power as Destiny*. New York: McGraw-Hill, 1968.

Epstein, I., ed. *The Babylonian Talmud*. 18 vols. London: Soncino, 1938.

Fairweather, W., and Black, J. S. *The First Book of Maccabees*. Cambridge: Cambridge U., 1897.

Farmer, William H. *Maccabees, Zealots and Josephus*. New York: Columbia U., 1956.

Flannery, Edward H. *The Anguish of the Jews*. New York: Macmillan, 1965.

Flemisch, Michael. *Grani Lieiniani*. Stuttgart: Teubneri, 1967.

Foster, B. O.; Moore, F. G.; Sage, Evan T.; and Schlesinger, A. C. *Livy*. Cambridge, Mass.: Harvard U., 1919-67.

Frazer, J. G. *Pausanias' Description of Greece*. Vol. 3. London: Macmillan, 1913.

Freedman, H., and Simon, Maurice. *Midrash Rabbah.* 10 vols. London: Soncino, 1951.

Friedlander, Gerald. *Pirkê De Rabbi Eliezer.* New York: Hermon, 1965.

Friedman, George. *The End of the Jewish People?* New York: Doubleday, 1967.

Fuller, John F. *The Generalship of Alexander the Great.* London: Eyre & Spottiswoode, 1958.

Ganneau, C. Clermont. "The Veil of the Temple of Jerusalem at Olympia," in *The Palestine Exploration Fund: Quarterly Statement for 1878.* London: Society Office, 1878.

Gaster, Theodor H. *The Dead Sea Scriptures.* Garden City, N.J.: Doubleday, 1957.

———. *Festivals of the Jewish Year.* New York: Sloane, 1968.

Gavran, Daniel. *The End of Days.* Philadelphia: Jewish Pubn. Soc., 1970.

Ginzberg, Louis. *The Legends of the Jews.* 7 vols. Philadelphia: Jewish Pubn. Soc., 1968.

Godley, A. D., trans. *Herodotus' Histories.* Cambridge, Mass.: Harvard U., 1920-25.

Golden, Hyman E. *The Book of Legends.* Vol. 3. New York: Hebrew Pubn., 1929.

Goldstein, Jonathan. *I Maccabees.* New York: Doubleday, 1976.

Gough, Richard. *Coins of the Seleucidae.* London: Nichols, 1803.

Graetz, H. *A Popular History of the Jews.* Vol. 1. New York: Hebrew Pubn., 1930.

Green, Peter. *Alexander the Great.* New York: Praeger, 1970.

Greenstone, Julius H. *The Messiah Idea in Jewish History.* Philadelphia: Jewish Pubn. Soc., 1948.

Griffith, G. T. *Alexander the Great: The Main Problems.* New York: Barnes & Noble, 1966.

———. *Hellenistic Civilization.* London: Arnold, 1953.

Gulick, Charles B. *The Deipnosophists.* 7 vols. New York: Putnam's, 1927-41.

Hadas, Moses. *The Third and Fourth Books of Maccabees.* New York: Harper, 1953.

Hengel, Martin. *Judaism and Hellenism.* Vol. 1. Philadelphia: Fortress, 1974.

188

In the Final Days

Hertz, J. H., ed. *The Pentateuch and Haftorahs.* London: Soncino, 1956.

Hillel, Abba. *A History of Messianic Speculation in Israel.* Boston: Smith, 1959.

Jones, H. L. *Strabo's Geography.* Cambridge, Mass.: Harvard U., 1917-32.

Jones, W. H. S.; Ormerod, H. A.; and Wycherly, R. E., trans. *Pausanias' Description of Greece.* New York: Putnam's, 1918-35.

Jouguest, Pierre. *Macedonian Imperialism and the Hellenization of the East.* New York: Knopf, 1928.

Keil, C. F. *Biblical Commentary on the Book of Daniel.* Grand Rapids: Eerdmans, 1949.

Ker, Walter C. A. *Cicero's Philippics.* New York: Putnam's, 1926.

Kincaid, C. A. "A Persian Prince—Antiochus Epiphanes," in *Oriental Studies in Honour of Cursetji Erachji Pavri.* Oxford: Oxford U., 1932.

Kincaid, C. A. *Successors of Alexander the Great.* Chicago: Argonaut, 1969.

Klausner, Joseph. *The Messianic Idea in Israel.* New York: Macmillan, 1955.

Kraeling, E. G. "Jewish Community in Antioch," *Journal of Biblical Literature* 51 (1932).

Learsi, Rufus. *Israel: A History of the Jewish People.* Cleveland: World, 1950.

Levin, Nora. *The Holocaust.* New York: Cromwell, 1968.

Mahaffy, John P. *Alexander's Empire.* London: Unwin, 1888.

———. *The Empire of the Ptolemies.* London: Macmillan, 1895.

———. *Greek Life and Thought from the Death of Alexander to the Roman Conquest.* London: Macmillan, 1896.

Margolis, Max, and Marx, Alexander. *A History of the Jewish People.* Philadelphia: Jewish Pubn. Soc., 1956.

Markholm, Otto. "The Accession of Antiochus IV of Syria," *The American Numismatic Society Museum Notes* 11 (1964).

———. *Antiochus IV of Syria.* Classical Et Mediaevalia. Diss. 8. Copenhagen: Gyldendalske Boghandel, 1966.

Maximon, Saadyah. *The Book of Hanukkah.* New York: Shulsinger, 1958.

McElroy, Neil. *The Second Book of Maccabees.* New York: Paulist, 1973.

Michener, James A. *The Source.* New York: Fawcett, 1967.

Mittwoch, A. "Tribute and Land Tax in Seleucid Judaea," *Biblica* 36 (1955).

Montefiore, C. G., and Lowe, H. *A Rabbinic Anthology.* New York: Schocken, 1974.

Montgomery, James A. *A Critical and Exegetical Commentary on the Book of Daniel.* The International Critical Commentary. Edinburgh: T. & T. Clark, 1927.

Moore, Clifford H. *Tacitus' Histories.* Cambridge, Mass.: Harvard U., 1914-37.

Murray, Steuben B. *Hellenistic Architecture in Syria.* Princeton: Princeton U., 1917.

Newman, Louis I. *The Hasidic Anthology.* New York: Schocken, 1972.

Nock, A. D. "Notes on Ruler Cult," *Journal of Hellenistic Studies* (1928).

Obermann, J. "The Sepulchre of the Maccabean Martyrs," *The Journal of Biblical Literature* 51 (1932) :250-65.

Oesterley, W. O. E., and Robinson, T. H. *A History of Israel.* Vol. 2. Oxford: Oxford U., 1932.

Oldfather, C. H.; Sherman, C. L.; Wells, C. Bradford; Greer, R. M.; and Walton, Francis, trans. *Diodorus Siculus Library of History.* 12 vols. Cambridge, Mass.: Harvard U., 1914-27.

Paton, W. R. *The Histories of Polybius.* Cambridge, Mass.: Harvard U., 1922-27.

Pearlman, Moshe. *The Maccabees.* New York: Macmillan, 1973.

Pearson, L. I. C. *The Lost Histories of Alexander the Great.* New York: Amer. Philological Assn., 1960.

Peters, Francis E. *The Harvest of Hellenism: A History of the Near East from Alexander the Great to the Triumph of Christianity.* New York: Simon & Schuster, 1971.

Phillips, Barry. "Antiochus IV Epiphanes," *The Journal of Biblical Literature* 29 (1910) :138 n.

Porter, Frank C. *The Message of the Apocalyptic Writers.* New York: Scribner's, 1905.

Price, Walter K. *The Coming Antichrist*. Chicago: Moody, 1974.

———. *Jesus' Prophetic Sermon*. Chicago: Moody, 1972.

———. *Next Year in Jerusalem*. Chicago: Moody, 1975.

———. *The Prophet Joel and the Day of the Lord*. Chicago: Moody, 1976.

———. "Tisha B'Av: A Day to Remember," *Christian Life*, July 1975.

Pusey, E. B. *Daniel the Prophet: Nine Lectures*. London: Innes, 1892.

Rackham, H., and Jones, W. H. S., trans. *Pliny's Natural History*. New York: Putnam's, 1938-.

Raddok, Charles. *Portrait of a People*. 3 vols. New York: Judaica, 1965.

Radin, Max L. *The Jews Among the Greeks and Romans*. Philadelphia: Jewish Pubn. Soc., 1915.

Reich, Rosalie. *Tales of Alexander the Macedonian: A Medieval Hebrew Manuscript*. New York: Ktav, 1972.

Reitlinger, Gerald. *The Final Solution*. New York: Yoselott, 1968.

Robinson, C. A. *Alexander the Great; The Meeting of East and West in World Government and Brotherhood*. New York: Dutton, 1947.

Robson, E. I., trans. *Arrian*. New York: Putnam's, 1929-33.

Rolf, John C. *Ammianus Marcellinus*. 3 vols. Cambridge, Mass.: Harvard U., 1935-39.

Rostortzeff, M. *The Social and Economic History of the Hellenistic World*. Oxford: Clarendon, 1941.

Roth, Cecil. *A Short History of the Jewish People*. London: East & West Lib., 1959.

Rowley, H. H. "Menelaus and the Abomination of Desolation," in *Studia Orientalia J. Pedersen Dicata*. Copenhagen, 1953.

———. *The Relevance of Apocalyptic*. New York: Association, 1964.

Russell, D. S. *The Jews from Alexander to Herod*. The Clarendon Bible. Vol. 5. Oxford: Oxford U., 1967.

Sachar, Abram. *A History of the Jews*. New York: Knoph, 1966.

Schalit, Abraham, ed. *The Hellenistic Age*. The World History of the Jewish People. Vol. 6. New Brunswick, N.J.: Rutgers U., 1972.

Schürer, Emil. *A History of the Jewish People in the Time of Jesus Christ.* New York: Scribner's, 1891.

Selincourt, Aubrey de, trans. *Flavius Arrianus' The Life of Alexander the Great.* London: Folio Soc., 1970.

Shakespeare, William. *Hamlet.*

Shepherd, R., trans. *Polyaenus' Strategemata.* 1793.

Shuckburgh, Evelyn. *The Histories of Polybius.* Vol. 2. London: Macmillan, 1889.

Silverman, Morris, and Silverman, Hillel. *Tisha B'Av Service.* Bridgeport, Conn.: Prayer Book Press, 1972.

Slotki, Judah J. *Daniel, Ezra, Nehemiah.* London: Soncino, 1970.

Snaith, Norman. *The Jews from Cyrus to Herod.* Surrey, England: Religious Educ., 1949.

Solis-Cohen, Emily. *Hanukkah: The Feast of Lights.* Philadelphia: Jewish Pubn. Soc., 1960.

Spinka, Matthew, and Downey, Glanville, trans. *Chronicle of John Malalas, Books VIII-XVIII.* Chicago: Chicago U., 1940.

Stevenson, William. *Strike Zion.* New York: Bantam, 1967.

Swain, J. W. "Antiochus Epiphanes and Egypt," *Classical Philology* 39 (1944) :73-94.

Tarn, W. W. *Alexander the Great.* Boston: Beacon, 1956.

———. *The Greeks in Bactria and India.* Cambridge: Cambridge U., 1938.

Tarn, W. W., and Griffith, G. T. *Hellenistic Civilization.* London: Arnold, 1953.

Tedesche, Sidney, and Zeitlin, Solomon. *The First Book of Maccabees.* New York: Harper, 1950.

———. *The Second Book of Maccabees.* New York: Harper, 1954.

Thackery, H. *Josephus' The Jewish Wars.* Cambridge, Mass.: Harvard U., 1927.

———. *Josephus' The Life and Against Apion.* Cambridge, Mass.: Harvard U., 1926.

Thackery, H.; Marcus, Ralph; Wikgren, Allen; and Feldman, L. H. *Josephus' Antiquities of the Jews.* Cambridge, Mass.: Harvard U., 1930-65.

Tcherikover, Victor. *Hellenistic Civilization of the Jews.* Philadelphia: Jewish Pubn. Soc., 1959.

Townshend, R. R. "Antiochus Epiphanes, the Brilliant Madman," *The Hubbert Journal,* Nov. 1913.

Uris, Leon. *Mila 18.* New York: Bantam, 1970.

Walbank, F. W. *A Historical Commentary on Polybius.* Oxford: Clarendon, 1957.

Walvoord, John F. *Daniel: The Key to Prophetic Revelation.* Chicago: Moody, 1971.

———. *Israel in Prophecy.* Grand Rapids: Zondervan, 1967.

———. *The Nations in Prophecy.* Grand Rapids: Zondervan, 1967.

Welles, Charles B. *Alexander and the Hellenistic World.* Toronto: Hakkert, 1970.

———. *Royal Correspondence in the Hellenistic Period.* Rome: L'Erma, 1966.

Wheeler, Benjamin I. *Alexander the Great; The Merging of East and West.* New York: Putnam's, 1900.

White, H. *Appian's Roman History.* 4 vols. Cambridge, Mass.: Harvard U., 1912-13.

Wiesel, Elie. *A Beggar in Jerusalem.* New York: Avon, 1971.

———. *The Oath.* New York: Random House, 1973.

———. *One Generation After.* New York: Random House, 1970.

Wilcken, Ulrich. *Alexander the Great.* New York: Borton, 1967.

Wilson, Robert Dick. *Studies in the Book of Daniel.* Vol. 2. Grand Rapids: Baker, 1972.

Wouk, Herman. *The Winds of War.* New York: Pocket Books, 1973.

Young, Edward J. *The Prophecy of Daniel.* Grand Rapids: Eerdmans, 1949.

Zeitlin, Solomon. "The Legend of the Ten Martyrs and Its Apocalyptic Origin," *Jewish Quarterly Review* (1945).

———. *The Rise and Fall of the Judean State.* 2 vols. Philadelphia: Jewish Pubn. Soc., 1968.

Zinberg, Israel. *A History of Jewish Literature.* Vol. 3. Philadelphia: Jewish Pubn. Soc., 1973.

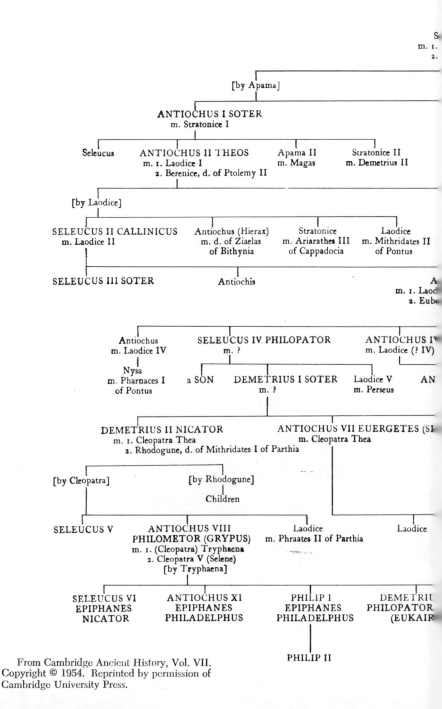